congregation). And [then revealed, you will win the conqueror's crown of glory.

—1 Peter 5:2–4, amp

Peter lays out some key tests for leaders in the church—tests that apply equally well in business. First, we need to hold our leadership positions willingly. Our mind-set should not be for what we can gain but rather for what we can add in serving others. We also need to guard against taking actions that relieve others from their responsibilities. We need to be overseers and not overdoers. Finally, we should focus on being a continual example, knowing we need to demonstrate the highest standard for ourselves. When we pass these tests, we receive true rewards from God.

Live It

- Discern your responsibilities and those of others; fulfill your responsibilities and help others fulfill theirs.

- Guard against focusing too much on WIIFM (what's in it for me); it's a natural tendency that will stunt your leadership results.

- Frequently evaluate your willingness to do what it takes to be a successful leader—and one who follows biblical principles—given your situation.

- Consider making a voluntary change if you find your willingness waning due to changes in direction, philosophy, policy, or personnel.

- Critically evaluate the degree to which you want others to follow your example—and ensure you hold the highest standard for yourself.

- Seek to be the leader others appreciate for effort and compassion as well as results.

- Seek to please God and to obtain His rewards, including the peace and joy that accompany passing these tests.

See It

Shortly into a new year, a series of events occurred that led to senior leader changes within my part of the business. At first, I was neutral about the changes, but soon the new leader ordered a series of actions I found myself wrestling with. I did not believe they were good business decisions, and they were difficult to implement while maintaining my group's performance from prior years. After thinking and praying about the changes, I realized I did not agree with many of them or with the underlying philosophy. I had to be honest with myself that my attitude was deteriorating, and I knew it would eventually become apparent and rub off on others. After praying and considering my options, I made the decision to transfer into another group even though I had to give up financial and career benefits to do it. It was a difficult decision but far easier than trying to "fake it." Eventually the changes were sorted out for the group, and I was on to a new phase of my career that would not have happened otherwise.

GUARD YOUR TRUST

The Passover commemorates the deliverance of the children of Israel from slavery in Egypt. Throughout His life, Jesus's custom was to go to Jerusalem to celebrate the Feast of Passover.

> But when He was in Jerusalem during the Passover Feast, many believed in His name [identified themselves with His party] after seeing His signs (wonders, miracles) which He was doing. But Jesus [for His part] did not trust Himself to them, because He knew all [men]; and He did not need anyone to bear witness concerning man [needed no evidence from anyone about men], for He Himself knew what was in human nature. [He could read men's hearts.]
> —John 2:23–25, AMP

Jesus was held in high regard at this time in His ministry. He had many friends. But He knew better than to open up to all His new friends—a caution to all of us who want to follow His wisdom. There are people who are friends for a reason, others for a season, and still others for a lifetime.

Be Leader-Ready

There are also others who may appear to be friends but may actually be focused on advancing or protecting themselves. Jesus was careful about whom He trusted and shows us we can be helpful to others and guard our trust at the same time.

Live It

- Recognize the importance of guarding confidences about yourself and your business endeavors; not everyone will be supportive.

- Pray and seek God's wisdom about how to obtain counsel— and from whom—and when to open confidences to others.

- Seek relationships with fellow believers in God, and realize that God may also expect you to build trusting relationships with others as well.

- Gain a mutual agreement with people; trust should go both ways.

- Be quick to receive and act on any "checks" you get in your spirit (discomfort that causes you to be uncertain or concerned); remember that the Holy Spirit always knows more than you do.

- Recognize the importance of evaluating relationships over time and as circumstances change; for instance, if you are promoted, some of your close relationships may need to change to reflect your new level of authority.

- Be sure you consistently demonstrate the characteristic of trustworthiness.

See It

"I just need to vent." A recently named general manager of a real estate company had called a family member to talk about a problem at the office. The "big boss" had just visited and made several comments that caused quite a stir among the staff. The general manager was concerned and a little angry.

LEAD AND SUCCEED

He started to say something to another person at the office but stopped himself. He wanted to sort out his thoughts and feelings, but in his new position, he just didn't know yet whom he could trust. So rather than risk making a bad decision in his new role, he reached out to someone he could trust—someone he knew wouldn't discuss it with anyone at the office. They chatted for a few minutes, and even though he knew she didn't understand the issue well, he felt better and was able to get back to work without feeling anxious.

A couple days later, they chatted again. "So, how do things look today?" The general manager was relieved to say everything was back to normal. The issues had died down, and he thanked her for being there when he needed a sounding board. He also thought to himself, "I'm sure glad I held my horses and didn't vent to someone on the staff. That could have been a real mess." The general manager had successfully guarded his trust in a new position and a vulnerable moment.

PRACTICE FLEXIBLE FOCUS

The Gospels indicate two instances where Jesus raised a person from the dead. This first episode happened at a time when many people knew of Jesus's power to heal, so crowds often followed Him as He traveled.

One day, a synagogue ruler named Jarius came to Jesus, begging Him to heal his daughter, who was at the point of death—and did die before Jesus reached her. But while Jesus was on His way, He was interrupted by someone else who needed healing.

> Now a certain woman had a flow of blood for twelve years, and had suffered many things from many physicians. She had spent all that she had and was no better, but rather grew worse. When she heard about Jesus, she came behind Him in the crowd and touched His garment; for she said, "If only I may touch His clothes, I shall be made well." Immediately the fountain of her blood was dried up, and she felt in her body that she was healed of the affliction. And Jesus, immediately knowing in Himself that power had gone out of Him, turned around in the crowd and said, "Who touched My clothes?"

Be Leader-Ready

But His disciples said to Him, "You see the multitude thronging You, and You say, 'Who touched Me?'" And He looked around to see her who had done this thing. But the woman, fearing and trembling, knowing what had happened to her, came and fell down before Him and told Him the whole truth. And He said to her, "Daughter, your faith has made you well. Go in peace, and be healed of your affliction."

...Wherever He entered, into villages, cities, or the country, they laid the sick in the marketplaces, and begged Him that they might just touch the hem of His garment. And as many as touched Him were made well.

—MARK 5:25–34; 6:56

Read the rest of the story in Mark 5:35–43.

Jesus was on His way to heal a gravely ill child—clearly an important task for His charter. (See Acts 10:38.) Time was of the essence, so it was necessary to focus on the task. When the "distraction" of the woman's healing happened, Jesus could have simply allowed her to get her healing and continue on His way. But instead, Jesus stopped and capitalized on the "distraction."

Focus is essential to be successful in business, but so is the art of knowing which "distractions" deserve immediate attention. To know when a "distraction" is really an opportunity that could be easily missed, you can use your mission or charter. And, of course, it is always valuable to listen to the still, small voice, which is frequently God speaking to us about what to do. Undoubtedly there were many other distractions in this crowd thronging Jesus. He was flexible to take the time to leverage the one distraction that provided a foundation for lasting value, as indicated a few verses later when others sought to touch His garment for healing.

Live It

- Prioritize your activities so you are spending your time and effort on what is most important.

LEAD AND SUCCEED

- Beware of the trap of "urgent"; often urgent issues are not important, but they can consume much time and attention.

- Recognize that important, valuable opportunities may present themselves at inopportune times.

- Seek God about how to engage these opportunities; He responds even to quick prayers, especially if we stay connected to Him in prayer on a regular basis.

- Consider what outcome would be beneficial and how much time is appropriate to devote to the "distraction" before returning to your focus task; notice Jesus sought for people to understand that it was her faith that made the woman well, knowing this vital truth would impact the thinking of others.

See It

I was "buried"—you know, the time when there are so many activities going on it is hard to know which one to work on next. And just then, an important opportunity presented itself. I was asked to do another training session on IBM's new Tangible Culture approach for consultants in Europe. The materials had been in place for two years, and the capabilities had advanced fairly significantly in some areas. The training in Europe would be with a fairly small team and in a country where I could not be sure we would gain a lot of market opportunity. Should I add to my own plate at a difficult time and update the materials? Or should I "slide by" with what we had and do my best to communicate the updated thinking in my course delivery? I chose to bite the bullet and make the updates, knowing I might be the only person who would really appreciate it.

Events rapidly proved it was a good decision—both for the company and for me personally. Two months after I delivered the new materials in Europe and found them to be far superior in helping people "get it," I was asked to take a new role at the company that would preclude me from doing future training. Others would need to shoulder the responsibility going forward. With the new materials in place, the transition to the new "teach team" was relatively quick and painless. I was able to move on to my new responsi-

10

Be Leader-Ready

bilities without dragging some of my old responsibilities with me or feeling guilty that I had not left the work in the best condition for others to use.

CONSIDER YOUR ROLE

Jesus frequently taught crowds of people, and often Pharisees and Sadducees were in the crowds. Sometimes these Jewish religious leaders were there for genuine reasons, and other times they were seeking to accuse Him. In this case, Jesus was eating at the house of a prominent Pharisee, and He used this opportunity to teach important lessons to those present.

> When you are invited by anyone to a wedding feast, do not sit down in the best place, lest one more honorable than you be invited by him; and he who invited you and him come and say to you, "Give place to this man," and then you begin with shame to take the lowest place. But when you are invited, go and sit down in the lowest place, so that when he who invited you comes he may say to you, "Friend, go up higher." Then you will have glory in the presence of those who sit at the table with you. For whoever exalts himself will be humbled, and he who humbles himself will be exalted.
> —Luke 14:8–11

In many business conference rooms, there are chairs at the table and around the perimeter of the room. When you attend a large meeting with many leaders, selecting the appropriate seat can be difficult. Higher position is typically the reason to select a seat at the table, but effective leaders will think beyond their position to their role in the meeting. If a junior person has a more active role, it shows both humility and a deep regard for the effectiveness of the outcome when you yield a seat at the table. This principle of considering your role, of course, goes beyond seats at meetings. It may actually be more important for your role on projects, teams, committees, and the like. The best leaders understand their roles are different in each of these situations and act accordingly.

LEAD AND SUCCEED

Live It

- Recognize you hold a position and that you also fulfill a series of roles, all of which come with differing levels and types of authority.

- Seek to understand who the authority is in each situation and how your role relates to the roles of others.

- Be sure to act appropriately with regard to the authority level you hold for particular roles, being careful not to equate position with role in all situations.

See It

Although I have held leader roles for a number of years, I have always relished doing the "real" work of culture transformation, organizational change management, and governance consulting. On several occasions, a person within my department has "hired" me to work as a subject matter expert or adviser on a project.

On one such occasion after working as an adviser for a few weeks, the project manager who "hired" me took me aside. She pointed out I was not consistently prompt to join team meetings, and it was disruptive to the team. She was right. I had let other priorities take precedence over my agreement to the team. In that setting, my role was to be a team member—not the boss. I apologized and amended my ways. And I learned an important lesson I have taught to others. As business becomes more complex, jobs are becoming more of a collection of roles than a singular position. The leaders who are quick to recognize their role and act accordingly will find the greatest success in an increasingly complex business environment.

CONCLUSION

Leadership is overall an awesome responsibility, not a privilege. To be a successful leader in business, each of us needs a lifestyle to build and maintain the right foundation for success. Although this takes time and effort, it is not only well worth it, but it is also pleasing to God as we seek His ways for our lives.

chapter two

ESTABLISH AND ASSIGN RESPONSIBILITIES

Distribute and coordinate work for collective results

O NE OF THE main reasons leaders are vital in business is because there are multiple ways to achieve goals. Without direction and coordination, different people are likely to choose different approaches, resulting in chaos. By establishing the needed structures and ordering the responsibilities, leaders help people to work together to achieve the requirements. Many business problems spring from issues in this vital area, so here is where you may really earn your pay!

RETAIN THE KEY DECISIONS ABOUT ORGANIZATIONAL STRUCTURE

This Scripture passage is a portion of Ezekiel's vision about the new city of Jerusalem and the new temple, specifically relating to the division of the land. It demonstrates the need for adequate details when it comes to ensuring people know their assignments.

> Now these are the names of the tribes: From the northern border along the road to Hethlon at the entrance of Hamath, to Hazar Enan, the border of Damascus northward, in the direction of Hamath, there shall be one section for Dan from its east to its west side; by the border of Dan, from the east side to the west, one section for Asher...by the border of Judah, from the east side to the west, shall be the district which you shall set apart, twenty-five thousand cubits in width, and in

length the same as one of the other portions, from the east side to the west, with the sanctuary in the center.

The district that you shall set apart for the LORD shall be twenty-five thousand cubits in length and ten thousand in width. To these—to the priests—the holy district shall belong: on the north twenty-five thousand cubits in length, on the west ten thousand in width, on the east ten thousand in width, and on the south twenty-five thousand in length. The sanctuary of the LORD shall be in the center....

Opposite the border of the priests, the Levites shall have an area twenty-five thousand cubits in length and ten thousand in width; its entire length shall be twenty-five thousand and its width ten thousand. And they shall not sell or exchange any of it; they may not alienate this best part of the land, for it is holy to the LORD.

The five thousand cubits in width that remain, along the edge of the twenty-five thousand, shall be for general use by the city, for dwellings and common-land; and the city shall be in the center.... The rest of the length, alongside the district of the holy section, shall be ten thousand cubits to the east and ten thousand to the west. It shall be adjacent to the district of the holy section, and its produce shall be food for the workers of the city. The workers of the city, from all the tribes of Israel, shall cultivate it. The entire district shall be twenty-five thousand cubits by twenty-five thousand cubits, foursquare. You shall set apart the holy district with the property of the city.

The rest shall belong to the prince, on one side and on the other of the holy district and of the city's property, next to the twenty-five thousand cubits of the holy district as far as the eastern border, and westward next to the twenty-five thousand as far as the western border, adjacent to the tribal portions; it shall belong to the prince. It shall be the holy district, and the sanctuary of the temple shall be in the center.

—EZEKIEL 48:1–2, 8–10, 13–15, 18–21

Establish and Assign Responsibilities

Read Ezekiel 48:1–29 to see all of God's detailed instructions.

This passage demonstrates God Himself making and communicating fairly detailed decisions about how to organize the people. Decisions about an organizational structure are best made by the top leaders and not left to the discretion of those involved. This is one exception to the general rule that more involvement is better. In fact, too much involvement in deciding the key aspects of any organizational structure is difficult because people often seek the best result for themselves personally. This can lead to slower decisions, strife, and even resistance to the final decisions. Instead, God shows us the best way to make these decisions: from the top and with enough detail to answer many questions about what "territory" belongs to whom. This approach gives appropriate high-level boundaries within which people may be given latitude for organizing and performing the details of their work (notice the more detailed decisions about how to organize within the "territories" are not documented here). By following God's example, you will bypass many of the problems that can accompany establishing organizational structures.

Live It

- Be sure you are clear about the vision, mission, and objectives for the organization before working on the structure to accomplish it.

- Identify the key characteristics needed for success, being sure to consider the history, culture, and business context.

- Develop design principles for the organizational structure:
    - What are the priorities among areas such as quality, innovation, and financial results?
    - What characteristics are important for the new structure (for example, standardization, flexibility, collaboration)?
    - How will people need to work together—within and between groups?
    - What leadership style is best suited to the future structure and way of working?

LEAD AND SUCCEED

- • What functions need to be covered, and what are their relative importance?
- • What elements from the past organizational structures should be retained? Modified? Eliminated?

- • Use the design principles to draft a high-level structure design—and involve a small number of leaders to refine and develop the structure after you have communicated their future roles to avoid jockeying for assignments.

- • Test your design against the design principles and against some realistic situations that may arise to ensure it will achieve the desired effect.

- • Identify the decisions you can delegate to others, being sure to clarify the boundaries of acceptable answers.

- • Consider the significance of the designed changes, and develop rollout and communication plans to help people move into the new structure. For example:
  - • How will the changes be perceived?
  - • What is the history of organizational changes for this group?
  - • Are there any natural events that will make these changes easier if done at the same time, such as year-end or combined with an upcoming project?
  - • Should you implement the new structure all at once or as two or more changes to help people adapt and adjust while fulfilling current responsibilities?
  - • Who should hear first, and how should the communications be cascaded to the rest of the organization?

See It

An executive of a large international company wanted to make some changes. It had been years since he had restructured his business unit, and some current issues necessitated some fairly radical changes. He understood

16

Establish and Assign Responsibilities

many of the changes he wanted to make would be met with concern and resistance, particularly among his top staff, so he chose to go it alone in designing the new structure. Rumors about pending changes were heating up, so members of his top staff approached him asking for information.

After holding them off several times, the executive finally spoke with each of his direct reports one-on-one to tell them about the changes. He concluded the conversations by saying, "These are the changes I've decided to make, so I need your support to carry them out." Even though several people wanted to discuss the changes in more detail—and wanted to understand the underlying reasons for some of his decisions—the executive simply told them to carry them out.

The top staff dutifully executed the changes, but there was a noticeable lack of enthusiasm. One major reason the leaders were not committed was the way the executive handled the change. No one was given the chance to raise even reasonable questions, let alone their concerns. Although the executive designed a good structure to address the organization's issues, he failed to solicit the support of his top staff and thus hurt some relationships. Ultimately, several important staff members chose to leave, and the organization's near-term results were lower than expected.

SHARE THE LEADERSHIP LOAD

Early in the Israelites' transition from Egypt to the Promised Land, Moses was confirmed in multiple situations as the leader of the people. In particular, he had led them from Egypt while God parted the Red Sea, miraculously brought food and water, and orchestrated a great victory against the Amalekites. The people trusted Moses, and they came to him to judge their disputes; so Moses had people standing before him from morning to night.

> So Moses' father-in-law said to him, "The thing that you do is not good. Both you and these people who are with you will surely wear yourselves out. For this thing is too much for you; you are not able to perform it by yourself. Listen now to my voice; I will give you counsel, and God will be with you: Stand before God for the people, so that you may bring the difficulties to God. And you shall teach them the statutes and the

LEAD AND SUCCEED

laws, and show them the way in which they must walk and the work they must do. Moreover you shall select from all the people able men, such as fear God, men of truth, hating covetousness; and place such over them to be rulers of thousands, rulers of hundreds, rulers of fifties, and rulers of tens. And let them judge the people at all times. Then it will be that every great matter they shall bring to you, but every small matter they themselves shall judge. So it will be easier for you, for they will bear the burden with you. If you do this thing, and God so commands you, then you will be able to endure, and all this people will also go to their place in peace."

So Moses heeded the voice of his father-in-law and did all that he had said. And Moses chose able men out of all Israel, and made them heads over the people: rulers of thousands, rulers of hundreds, rulers of fifties, and rulers of tens. So they judged the people at all times; the hard cases they brought to Moses, but they judged every small case themselves.

—Exodus 18:17–26

The "best" leader to make decisions may not be the best choice. In this instance, Moses was the best leader because he had the "inside track" to God's will, which the people sought. But his personal involvement in all decisions led to delays, frustration, and—perhaps even more important—a missed opportunity to develop leadership and decision-making capabilities in others. Notice the first step was to teach the people the requirements. This would enable them to handle more on their own. Then leaders were given authority over small to large responsibilities and guidelines for escalating difficult decisions. Follow this biblical example and enable others to grow capabilities for the good of the organization and their own careers—and free your schedule to engage in the most important decisions and actions.

Live It

- Remember you are not expected—nor should you try—to do it all.

Establish and Assign Responsibilities

- Look actively for opportunities to involve and empower others to make decisions and take action.

- Design an approach with the following principles:
  - Identify scope and boundaries for the delegated responsibilities so it is clear when people should and should not take action.
  - Prepare people for the responsibilities through communication, education, and training so they have the needed knowledge and skills.
  - Be available to help if requested—but resist the temptation to "jump in" too quickly; people develop most effectively when they have to think and learn for themselves.
  - Provide coaching, especially when results have fallen short or mistakes have been made.

- Implement your approach, being sure to:
  - Recognize that delegating authority and responsibility means you have agreed to accept the fact that mistakes will occur, so address those mistakes from that mind-set.
  - Resist the urge to overturn decisions because it may effectively disempower both the original decision maker and everyone who hears about it.
  - Apply prayer and wisdom to know the fine balance between allowing people to learn through their mistakes and correcting the mistakes that need to be corrected.

See It

The leader of a department wanted to establish a new way of working. She knew it was important to share responsibility to get the work done effectively, so she worked with her leadership team to organize several specific cross-departmental responsibilities.

However, two factors came into play that eventually crippled her plans. First, the cross-departmental responsibilities were on complex topics, so

19

it was difficult to set effective boundaries. Second, she was an admitted perfectionist and often overturned decisions others had made. This led some people to avoid making decisions, opting instead to escalate them to the leader for fear of making a mistake or being publicly overturned. Others would make the "decisions" but did not spend much time thinking them through because they expected the decisions to be overturned and didn't want to waste effort.

The leader quickly found herself reviewing almost everything and was frustrated that her attempts to delegate had not succeeded. In her eagerness to ensure excellent results, she had violated several key principles necessary to effectively share the load. The boundaries of decision authority were not clear, and she frequently overturned decisions rather than accepting many and using all as learning experiences. In the end, her team was demoralized, and several top performers chose to move on with their careers, feeling they had few opportunities to develop within the department.

BE WILLING TO CONSIDER THE UNEXPECTED CANDIDATE

This situation happened early in Jesus's ministry on Earth. Levi (also called Matthew) was one of Jesus's disciples eventually chosen to be one of the twelve apostles. Before he became a disciple, he was a tax collector—a position known for dishonesty and largely reviled in that day.

> After these things He went out and saw a tax collector named Levi, sitting at the tax office. And He said to him, "Follow Me." So he left all, rose up, and followed Him. Then Levi gave Him a great feast in his own house. And there were a great number of tax collectors and others who sat down with them. And their scribes and the Pharisees complained against His disciples, saying, "Why do You eat and drink with tax collectors and sinners?" Jesus answered and said to them, "Those who are well have no need of a physician, but those who are sick. I have not come to call the righteous, but sinners, to repentance."
>
> —LUKE 5:27–32

Establish and Assign Responsibilities

Jesus made an unusual and unexpected choice in this situation. Matthew was not the expected profile for a successful disciple. But Jesus's choice clearly opened the door to His mission extending in a new and different direction—into the realm of the tax collectors and other sinners Jesus needed to reach. When it comes to making assignments, it is important for you to pray and follow God's leading, which is often indicated by the decision that feels peaceful on the inside. When you are confident you have made God's selection, there is no need to be concerned over what others think about the decision. God will always support the decisions that align with His will.

Live It

♦ Approach the process of making assignments with an open mind.

♦ Consider a broad range of characteristics:
  ♦ Capabilities, knowledge, and skills
  ♦ Previous experience
  ♦ Lessons the candidates may have learned—perhaps the hard way
  ♦ Relationships with others and how this could open or close opportunities necessary for the position
  ♦ Reputation
  ♦ Character

♦ Seek the input of others about the candidates you are considering.

♦ Seek God in prayer before you finalize your decision.

♦ Be willing to make an unexpected assignment; you may find unexpected benefits.

See It

One heavy manufacturing company was experiencing tremendous problems. Competitive pressures and changes in the industry had put it on the brink of bankruptcy. Several activities were underway to save the company and the jobs this primary employer brought to the small community.

One of the efforts involved a significant redesign of the manufacturing support processes to identify cost savings and enable fewer people to fulfill the requirements. As the consultants brought in to facilitate the redesign, we worked with the company to assemble a team of people familiar with the current processes. Among the team members was a very unlikely selection. Few knew him, which meant he did not fit the profile of credible advocates we requested. But when the project sponsor questioned whether he should join the team, his manager was adamant he was the right person. During the project, this man proved to be insightful, creative, and very eager to do whatever was necessary for the company's success. After the final presentation—where this man was selected to be one of the presenters—the sponsor remarked he was a diamond in the rough. His manager deserves a lot of credit for the team's success by ensuring the man was selected for that important assignment.

REMIND LOWER LEADERS OF THEIR RESPONSIBILITIES

Shortly after Solomon's death, a split separated the Israelites into two kingdoms: Judah and Israel. Jehoshaphat was one of the kings in Judah. He was a good king who sought to do God's will.

> So Jehoshaphat dwelt at Jerusalem; and he went out again among the people from Beersheba to the mountains of Ephraim, and brought them back to the LORD God of their fathers. Then he set judges in the land throughout all the fortified cities of Judah, city by city, and said to the judges, "Take heed to what you are doing, for you do not judge for man but for the LORD, who is with you in the judgment. Now therefore, let the fear of the LORD be upon you; take care and do it, for there is no iniquity with the LORD our God, no partiality, nor taking of bribes."
>
> Moreover in Jerusalem, for the judgment of the LORD and for controversies, Jehoshaphat appointed some of the Levites and priests, and some of the chief fathers of Israel, when they

Establish and Assign Responsibilities

returned to Jerusalem. And he commanded them, saying, "Thus you shall act in the fear of the LORD, faithfully and with a loyal heart: Whatever case comes to you from your brethren who dwell in their cities, whether of bloodshed or offenses against law or commandment, against statutes or ordinances, you shall warn them, lest they trespass against the LORD and wrath come upon you and your brethren. Do this, and you will not be guilty. And take notice: Amariah the chief priest is over you in all matters of the LORD; and Zebadiah the son of Ishmael, the ruler of the house of Judah, for all the king's matters; also the Levites will be officials before you. Behave courageously, and the LORD will be with the good."

—2 CHRONICLES 19:4–11

Jehoshaphat set up lower-level leaders—judges—in the cities of Judah. In giving them their authority, he made it clear they needed to fulfill their responsibilities in a way that honored God as their ultimate "Boss"—and be responsible to additional leaders for different arenas of their work. His words also conveyed the importance of their positions and the decisions they would make for the good of the people. As leaders, one of our responsibilities is to lead the leaders under us and to oversee how they fulfill their leadership responsibilities. This passage contains many of the needed reminders and is a good one for you to follow in establishing and confirming those responsibilities. Also, be sure to reinforce both the responsibilities you expect them to fulfill and the way you want them to do their work, such as acting with integrity and courage.

Live It

- Meet with leaders under your responsibility and discuss your philosophy and values; these expectations can be the most important over time.

- Reinforce that leadership is a responsibility and not a privilege.

23

LEAD AND SUCCEED

- Role-model your philosophy and values so others can see a good example—and make coaching and teaching a regular part of your interactions.

- Warn the leaders of the difficulties they may face, and give them instructions and ideas on what to do.

- Encourage and support their efforts as well as results.

- Recognize their successes openly and frequently—and show appreciation often.

See It

In my leadership roles, I attempt to be transparent: communicating the successes and struggles of our business so we can enjoy and work on them together. At the beginning of one year, I was asked to consolidate several teams into my existing department—a move that more than doubled its size overnight and added the challenge of learning to work together. That year, our team significantly outperformed all of its objectives, and most people had met or exceeded their primary individual objective, so expectations for good performance ratings were high. But because the rest of our business unit had struggled, we were faced with the sober reality of doling out fewer top scores and more low scores than we felt were appropriate.

I met with the leadership team to discuss the difficult task we faced. The leaders needed a thorough understanding of the challenge to both communicate it to their teams and to avoid the protective mentality that often accompanies the rating process. When we held our discussion about performance across the entire department, the benefit of ensuring the leaders understood the challenge paid off. We were able to quickly identify people "on the bubble"—the ones who were candidates for higher or lower scores. We also were open in our discussions about each person, which helped me to advocate effectively for the proper scores as we consolidated results across the business unit and made final rating decisions. In the end, the overall performance of my group was recognized, and we were able to move some of the "bubble" candidates up to the higher scores. Together, the leaders of this group fulfilled a key responsibility during a challenging time and

Establish and Assign Responsibilities

demonstrated the values and dedication that led to the great performance that year.

MITIGATE THE EFFECTS OF ONEROUS TASKS

The following situation occurred as King Solomon began the task of building the temple. There was peace between Israel and surrounding kingdoms at this time, including Tyre.

> So the LORD gave Solomon wisdom, as He had promised him; and there was peace between Hiram and Solomon, and the two of them made a treaty together.
>
> Then King Solomon raised up a labor force out of all Israel; and the labor force was thirty thousand men. And he sent them to Lebanon, ten thousand a month in shifts: they were one month in Lebanon and two months at home; Adoniram was in charge of the labor force.
>
> —1 KINGS 5:12–14

Notice Solomon sent people away from home to work for a month, but he gave them two months at home between work shifts. If people are asked to do something difficult, it is important to mitigate the negative aspects. Otherwise, people may resent the expectations and their loyalty can decrease. If people know you care about their situation, they are more willing to do the difficult work you need them to do. Here, Solomon shows us some of his God-given wisdom in leading people.

Live It

- Talk with others to understand the nature of the assignment from the perspective of those who need to perform it.

- Recognize you may have a higher threshold for difficulty; just because you do not think something is onerous does not mean others will share your view.

- Work with others to identify ways to mitigate the most difficult aspects of the work.

LEAD AND SUCCEED

- Monitor the decisions you have made over time to ensure they are having the desired effect.

- Recognize that you may have to make adjustments for unforeseen circumstances.

- Remember the value of appreciation, and thank people for their extra efforts.

See It

I have learned it is important to build relationships with people so they feel free to indicate their preferences, especially about the heavy travel associated with consulting. Although some people are forthcoming with their preferences, others are reticent for fear of coming across as having a willingness or attitude issue.

For one long-term engagement in South Korea, I needed people from North America who would agree to six months overseas on a cycle of three weeks away, then one week home. I spoke with many candidates to determine who would be willing and able to meet the travel requirements. As the work began, we assisted each person with his or her own particular needs, including temporarily moving one consultant's wife and infant son to Seoul to be with him. I also made an extended visit to launch the work and establish regular communications to support it going forward. Because of the time zone difference, I often communicated with the team at difficult hours in the States. However, this combination of extra effort on all sides paid off in a successful client project and in high employee satisfaction.

CONCLUSION

Leaders, by the essence of their role, coordinate the effective work of others. This requires establishing and organizing both the work and the associated responsibilities. By following the Bible's examples, you will be better able to make the right decisions and take the right actions for results. When people and their work are well organized and coordinated, morale is higher and business results are easier to achieve.

chapter three

SELECT THE RIGHT LEADERS
Choose leaders through wisdom and understanding

L EADERS OFTEN HAVE the responsibility of selecting leaders to work under them—and in today's matrix business structures, they may even have a role in selecting peers and their own leaders. The larger the organization, the more important this responsibility becomes because layers of leadership add distance between people and introduce the risk of inconsistency. The Bible mentions the topic of leader selection in many places. These lessons are also good reminders and tests to evaluate ourselves for the promotions and advanced positions we may seek.

ACCEPT GOD'S CHOSEN LEADER
This episode occurred late in King David's life, shortly before his son Solomon was anointed as his successor. David wanted to build the first permanent temple for God, but God told David that Solomon would build it.

> Then King David rose to his feet and said, "Hear me, my brethren and my people: I had it in my heart to build a house of rest for the ark of the covenant of the LORD, and for the footstool of our God, and had made preparations to build it. But God said to me, 'You shall not build a house for My name, because you have been a man of war and have shed blood.' However the LORD God of Israel chose me above all the house of my father to be king over Israel forever, for He has chosen Judah to be the ruler; and of the house of Judah, the house of my father, and among the sons of my father, He was pleased with me to make me king over all Israel.

27

LEAD AND SUCCEED

And of all my sons (for the LORD has given me many sons)
He has chosen my son Solomon to sit on the throne of the
kingdom of the LORD over Israel. Now He said to me, 'It is
your son Solomon who shall build My house and My courts;
for I have chosen him to be My son, and I will be his Father.
Moreover I will establish his kingdom forever, if he is stead-
fast to observe My commandments and My judgments, as
it is this day.' Now therefore, in the sight of all Israel, the
assembly of the LORD, and in the hearing of our God, be
careful to seek out all the commandments of the LORD your
God, that you may possess this good land, and leave it as an
inheritance for your children after you forever.

"As for you, my son Solomon, know the God of your
father, and serve Him with a loyal heart and with a willing
mind; for the LORD searches all hearts and understands all
the intent of the thoughts. If you seek Him, He will be found
by you; but if you forsake Him, He will cast you off forever.
Consider now, for the LORD has chosen you to build a house
for the sanctuary; be strong, and do it."

...And David said to his son Solomon, "Be strong and of
good courage, and do it; do not fear nor be dismayed, for the
LORD God—my God—will be with you. He will not leave
you nor forsake you, until you have finished all the work
for the service of the house of the LORD. Here are the divisions of the priests and the Levites for all the service of the
house of God; and every willing craftsman will be with you
for all manner of workmanship, for every kind of service;
also the leaders and all the people will be completely at your
command."

—1 CHRONICLES 28:2–10, 20–21

David gave Solomon some specific instructions for building the temple—
read about them in 1 Chronicles 28:11–19.

David had prepared for the building of the temple. But God chose another
to lead the work: Solomon. As with Moses and Joshua in different stages of

Select the Right Leaders

leading the Israelites out of Egypt and through the wilderness into the Promised Land, there are times for a change in leadership. Those of us who want to do God's will in the workplace need to be discerning of God's choices and timing. David, without hesitation, prepared materials and plans and mentored Solomon to take over his position as God desired. He constructively handled a situation that could have been difficult and emotional. It is a positive example for all of us—and a reminder we may face a similar challenge in our own careers someday: the challenge of giving up a desired leadership position to another.

Live It

- Recognize the benefit of different types of leaders in different circumstances; their strengths and style can either be an asset or a hindrance depending on the situation.

- Listen to your heart; God may be giving you insights into changing conditions that may not be apparent yet, or He may have a new assignment for you and others.

- Remember God will recognize and reward what you have done to promote His purposes, even when the decisions and actions may be difficult for you.

- If you need to turn over your role to a new leader, actively seek to promote his or her success:
    - Advocate and openly communicate your support for the new leader.
    - Make needed preparations to support future success.
    - Mentor and encourage the new leader.

See It

A few years ago, I had to deal with "losing" a leadership position due to a major restructuring. Before the final decisions were announced, I prayed and let God know about my desires to continue in the role but submitted those desires to God's will. When my boss told me I was not selected, I was disappointed but decided to support the decision, believing it was God's will.

29

LEAD AND SUCCEED

But the really hard part was yet to come: doing *all* I could to propel the new leader to success. It would have been very easy to do only the minimum and not be completely proactive in assisting him. But I chose to watch my attitude and prioritized the actions I believed would help him—and others—through the transition. I'm glad I did. The two of us eventually became close colleagues, and his support was instrumental in a position I accepted shortly thereafter—a position that proved to be pivotal in my career and one I might not have accepted under different circumstances. God wanted to move me in another direction, and He made that very clear with the answer to my prayer. Rather than looking back on this time as a "loss," I now see it as the launch point to a new stage of my career.

PRIORITIZE CHARACTER IN SELECTING LEADERS

Timothy was a protégé of the apostle Paul during the early days of the Christian church. Paul wrote two letters to Timothy that provide guidance on building a strong organization, which in Timothy's case was a church.

> This is a faithful saying: If a man desires the position of a bishop, he desires a good work. A bishop then must be blameless, the husband of one wife, temperate, sober-minded, of good behavior, hospitable, able to teach; not given to wine, not violent, not greedy for money, but gentle, not quarrelsome, not covetous; one who rules his own house well, having his children in submission with all reverence (for if a man does not know how to rule his own house, how will he take care of the church of God?); not a novice, lest being puffed up with pride he fall into the same condemnation as the devil. Moreover he must have a good testimony among those who are outside, lest he fall into reproach and the snare of the devil.
>
> —1 TIMOTHY 3:1–7

The requirements Paul set forth for selecting leaders in the church are also the types of characteristics we should seek in selecting leaders for business. Why? Paul bases his instructions on the notion that leaders must first

Select the Right Leaders

be good at handling themselves and other small groups before they are ready for more—a solid standard with obvious benefits. Notice Paul does not primarily focus on the capabilities for the work. He seems to assume Timothy will naturally consider them. Instead, he advises Timothy to look beyond the obvious to the indications of the person's character. Consider Paul's characteristics for leaders:

- Positive and solid track record for leadership

- Known for good behavior and self-control

- Able to teach others

- Focused on achieving results through others

- Well regarded by others

- Not focused on obtaining personal gain

- Known for integrity and character both on the job and in their personal lives

Live It

- Develop a list of the specific knowledge and skills needed to perform the work.

- Consider the nature of the leadership position.
  - Will the leader need to lead a small or large group?
  - Will the leader need to influence others outside that department?
  - What were the characteristics of the last leader, and to what degree were they successful?
  - Is the job changing in a way that will modify the leader requirements?

- Develop a list of specific character traits for performing the job effectively; for example:
  - Needs to be known for building consensus and working collaboratively with others

31

LEAD AND SUCCEED

- Needs to demonstrate confidence even in the face of
  uncertainty
- Needs to know how to speak frankly and candidly, yet
  with sensitivity

- Discuss the desired character traits with others to clarify and
  prioritize what is needed.

- Develop questions to test the degree to which these traits
  are present in the candidates, focusing on questions to solicit
  specific examples from their past.

- Be aware that how you ask the questions is very important; the candidates may pick up on your priorities and say
  what you want to hear if you imply the right answer (for
  example, "Tell me of a situation where you needed to build
  consensus.").

- Be sure to check references, including former subordinates,
  to validate and augment what your leading candidates have
  told you.

See It

In a manufacturer's finance department, a new manager was brought in
to lead an intact group. During the interview process, the executive told
her about a supervisor who was extremely knowledgeable and would be
a great asset as the manager sought to learn the details. After starting
her position, it became clear to the manager that the supervisor was tech-
nically competent, but she was a poor leader. The supervisor frequently
failed to make herself available when people needed help and would say
things easily interpreted as "put-downs" (for example, "Why don't you
know this?").

To fill the leadership void caused by this supervisor's approach, people
would ask another peer for assistance—someone who was constructive and
helpful, even though it required going beyond her regular job duties. The
new manager had a difficult choice: allow an ineffective leader to stay in

Select the Right Leaders

a key role or make difficult and emotional changes to improve the functioning of the group.

After wrestling with multiple options, the manager chose to promote the informal leader to an additional supervisor position and divided the team into two groups. People were then assigned to the supervisors based on their experience levels. Before she announced the changes, she spoke privately to the original supervisor and candidly explained the changes and why they were being made. She also offered to coach and mentor her to become a more effective leader—an offer the supervisor accepted. The supervisor received the message: her stature in the group had gone down, and she would need to develop her leadership skills to advance in her career. The promotion of the informal leader was well received by others in the department, and it reinforced the collaborative environment the new manager wanted to encourage. In a short time, the organization's results and morale improved.

CONSIDER THE VALUE OF SIMILAR EXPERIENCE

Hebrews is a book in the New Testament originally written for Christians of Jewish descent. Its authorship is not certain, but it may have been Paul, Barnabas, Apollos, or another associate of Paul.

> Inasmuch then as we have a great High Priest Who has [already] ascended and passed through the heavens, Jesus the Son of God, let us hold fast our confession [of faith in Him]. For we do not have a High Priest Who is unable to understand and sympathize and have a shared feeling with our weaknesses and infirmities and liability to the assaults of temptation, but One Who has been tempted in every respect as we are, yet without sinning. Let us then fearlessly and confidently and boldly draw near to the throne of grace (the throne of God's unmerited favor to us sinners), that we may receive mercy [for our failures] and find grace to help in good time for every need [appropriate help and well-timed help, coming just when we need it].
>
> —HEBREWS 4:14–16, AMP

LEAD AND SUCCEED

This passage explains a vital characteristic of Jesus: He had experienced the challenges of living as a human being. Applying this truth to a business setting, we can conclude leaders who have similar experiences to those they lead can be more effective in many situations. This is not an overriding requirement, and you may instead need a leader who will bring change. But people are often more likely to feel comfortable with someone who has "been there." This can make it easier to accept the new leader and can cause others to learn more readily from him or her. As you think about your selection criteria, consider similar experience and background and their potential value.

Live It

- Consider the nature of the work.
  - How complex is it?
  - How long does it take to learn and be proficient?
  - How experienced is the current staff, and is attrition an issue?
  - What types of issues will the leader need to address?
  - What types of support will the leader need to provide to the people?
  - How important has detailed experience been to the success of previous leaders?
  - Are there others, including those at higher and lower levels, who can teach a new leader what he or she needs to know?
- Identify and understand any changes the leader will need to implement in the new role.
- Consider the impact of a promotion from within the group versus bringing in a "new perspective."
  - Promotions can be a significant motivator and morale boost, but they can breed "groupthink" (where people think too much alike) and competitive strife during and after the selection process.

Select the Right Leaders

- People from outside the department or company can help to create the dynamics for change but are likely to lack an understanding of the work details and culture—and their selection may demotivate internal candidates or cause them to question their advancement opportunities.

See It

The combined leadership team for a recent merger was struggling on multiple fronts, and I was asked to facilitate the team through some pivotal decisions where the leaders had strong differences of opinion. I used a technique called Right vs. Right, which helps leaders choose between multiple valid options often at the source of culture clash and other conflicts.[1]

One of the conflicts centered on expectations for leaders. One of the companies had historically expected its leaders to be "people leaders"— leaders who were expected to focus on overall business results and what needed to be done to enable people to produce those results. In their model, leaders were not necessarily experienced in the subject areas they led. They described their model as an "empowered" model. The other company had a different view. They felt the leaders needed strong capabilities in the areas they led—enough to be able to jump in and perform the work when needed. Although they admitted some of their leaders neglected the "people" requirements at times, they knew the work was always done to a high standard, and people were actively mentored through working side-by-side with the leaders. These were two right answers—and very strong opinions on both sides about which one would be best.

As we worked through the constructive dialogue promoted through the Right vs. Right technique, the leaders began to see they needed both models to be most effective. Of course, they wanted to take action to promote high employee satisfaction. Also, the business plan called for rapid growth where it would be valuable for leaders to perform the work at times and be able to make decisions from a detailed understanding recognized by the people. In the end, the leaders decided on a blended model slightly "tipped" toward leaders experienced with the detailed work. The leader model was later tailored within each department to the detailed responsibilities. The result:

LEAD AND SUCCEED

an area of strife was leveraged into an opportunity to apply the best of both companies.

USE GOD'S SELECTION CRITERIA

This episode occurred shortly after the first king of Israel, Saul, committed a great sin of rebellion toward God. Samuel, the prophet and spiritual leader at the time, then received a message from God that Saul was rejected as king. God instructed Samuel to anoint God's new chosen king from the family of Jesse.

> So Samuel did what the LORD said, and went to Bethlehem. And the elders of the town trembled at his coming, and said, "Do you come peaceably?" And he said, "Peaceably; I have come to sacrifice to the LORD. Sanctify yourselves, and come with me to the sacrifice." Then he consecrated Jesse and his sons, and invited them to the sacrifice.
>
> So it was, when they came, that he looked at Eliab and said, "Surely the LORD's anointed is before Him." But the LORD said to Samuel, "Do not look at his appearance or at the height of his stature, because I have refused him. For the LORD does not see as man sees; for man looks at the outward appearance, but the LORD looks at the heart." So Jesse called Abinadab, and made him pass before Samuel. And he said, "Neither has the LORD chosen this one." Then Jesse made Shammah pass by. And he said, "Neither has the LORD chosen this one." Thus Jesse made seven of his sons pass before Samuel. And Samuel said to Jesse, "The LORD has not chosen these." And Samuel said to Jesse, "Are all the young men here?" Then he said, "There remains yet the youngest, and there he is, keeping the sheep." And Samuel said to Jesse, "Send and bring him. For we will not sit down till he comes here." So he sent and brought him in. Now he was ruddy, with bright eyes, and good-looking. And the LORD said, "Arise, anoint him; for this is the one!" Then Samuel took the horn of oil and anointed him in the

36

Select the Right Leaders

midst of his brothers; and the Spirit of the LORD came upon David from that day forward. So Samuel arose and went to Ramah.

—1 SAMUEL 16:4–13

When selecting someone to lead others, we need to be sensitive to God's guidance. We cannot see a person's heart, but God can. We cannot know how people will interact with each other, but He does. In other words, any selection we make in our own knowledge and wisdom can prove to be a failure. But any choice we put in God's hands, agreeing to follow His desire, will be successful—even if it seems unusual or gets off to a rocky start. God will direct our decisions if we let Him.

Live It

+ Be sure to start every major "people" decision with prayer.

+ Be determined to find God's will for that situation.

+ Let God's peace be the key criterion as you consider the candidates.

+ Be willing to delay the selection process if you have not found peace; you may not have seen the right one yet.

+ Pray for the leader you have selected—for success in results and relationships and for God's will and blessing.

See It

One day at lunch, a leader with one of my clients shared a story about a particular internal support group she had contacted to help her with an important meeting. When she called to request changes—changes required to meet her *original* request—she was met with a hostile response. She told me with obvious frustration, "And this is not the first time. They treat everyone this way, even when it is their mistake. We can't make these things happen ourselves, but they give us a lot of grief when we ask them to do it. What do they expect? Seems like they think their function is the hub of this company. And they're *all* like that—especially the leader."

37

LEAD AND SUCCEED

With those last three words, I knew she had identified the source of the problem. As I found out later when others shared similar stories, the group's leader was exceptional for one very important requirement. But he was very inflexible for the rest of the work, which included day-to-day interactions with others in the company—and he had hired people just like himself. As I worked with this client over a period of months, I was amazed at how many problems pointed back to this leader, his style, and the problematic team he had assembled—and how some at the company felt they were "held hostage" because he was good at only one important task.

MAKE NO HASTY LEADERSHIP APPOINTMENTS

This episode happened fairly early in Jesus's three-year ministry. At this point, He already had a sizable following of disciples.

> Now it came to pass in those days that He went out to the mountain to pray, and continued all night in prayer to God. And when it was day, He called His disciples to Himself; and from them He chose twelve whom He also named apostles: Simon, whom He also named Peter, and Andrew his brother; James and John; Philip and Bartholomew; Matthew and Thomas; James the son of Alphaeus, and Simon called the Zealot; Judas the son of James, and Judas Iscariot who also became a traitor.
>
> —LUKE 6:12–16

Jesus had called many of His disciples specifically (see Mark 1:16–20, 2:14), but the leadership appointments to positions of the twelve apostles did not come until some time had passed. Hasty leadership appointments—ones made without both prayer and experience with the person—can be trouble. In this case, these leaders had significant future responsibilities, so it was critical that Jesus make the right decisions the first time. Jesus sought the Father's direction in prayer to make the right leader decisions, so we should not believe we can do a better job on our own. Take the time you need to experience God's peace about selecting leaders, and you'll be glad you did.

Select the Right Leaders

Live It

- Be sure to seek God in prayer—first and foremost.

- Allow some time to get to know the candidates personally before making decisions.

- Recognize candidates come with strengths and weaknesses— and also history, experiences, preferences, relationships, interests, and other critical dimensions to be considered.

- Consider when it is best to communicate your decision criteria, knowing it could influence candidates to "sell you" or even drop out, but it could also lead you to receive important information you may need to know.

- After making your decisions, communicate the reasons to the person chosen, other candidates, and people who will work with and for the person you chose; it can reinforce your priorities and help position the new leader for success.

See It

Following an organization restructure, I inherited a number of new people into my team—both individuals and intact teams. Within the integrated department, there was a group of people at the leader level, some of who already had teams of various sizes, while others were individual contributors. One of our first activities as a leadership team was to assign people to the leaders and dole out other responsibilities for planning, managing, and measuring the work. We wanted to share the load and leverage everyone's strengths and preferences. In making the assignments, we discussed:

- Existing relationships between leaders and those they previously led

- Capabilities, experience, and preferences

- Location, because the team was spread across the United States

LEAD AND SUCCEED

- Nature of the client projects and other work responsibilities for the foreseeable future

- Growth and development plans for each individual and for the team as a whole

I spoke with each leader individually—and with the collective team—to understand their views about the changes. I also prayed about making the best choices for everyone involved because I knew the change was disruptive and difficult for some. In the end, we assigned some leaders with more "people" responsibilities and others with more management system responsibilities, according to what best suited their capabilities and interests and the growth planned for that year.

Later in the year—and very unexpectedly—I was asked to lead a critical project. I would be absent for four months and needed the leadership team to handle things on their own during that time. One of the leaders who had been performing many of the overall management system tasks quickly stepped into the lead role, and everyone continued to perform without a hiccup. In fact, that year the team produced outstanding results, and I believe God helped us to order things in the best way possible so my unexpected assignment did not interrupt the team's functioning.

CONCLUSION

Leaders often lead other leaders, and selecting the right ones can make all the difference between an organization set for success and one that is mediocre on its best day. Use the Bible's wisdom to help guide your selection of leaders, and be well on your way to decisions you will be proud to admit.

chapter four

CLARIFY AUTHORITY

Prevent problems through proper power structures

AUTHORITY IS AN important biblical concept, and it is vital to understand and honor it in every aspect of life, including business. Unfortunately, rebellion and questioning of authority are common today—and they are damaging in many ways. This chapter bases itself on Romans 13:1, which says: "Let every soul be subject to the governing authorities. For there is no authority except from God, and the authorities that exist are appointed by God." To be effective—and at peace—in our business leadership roles, we need to see authority as God sees it and handle authority as He intends it to be handled.

DISCERN THE AUTHORITY

Peter and Paul were apostles and leaders in the early Christian church. Peter was one of the original twelve disciples who walked with Jesus. Paul, originally named Saul, met Jesus after His ascension through the miraculous encounter documented in Acts 9:1–22. Paul is the writer of the following passage.

> Then after fourteen years I went up again to Jerusalem with Barnabas, and also took Titus with me. And I went up by revelation, and communicated to them that gospel which I preach among the Gentiles, but privately to those who were of reputation, lest by any means I might run, or had run, in vain....
>
> But on the contrary, when they saw that the gospel for the uncircumcised had been committed to me, as the gospel for

41

LEAD AND SUCCEED

the circumcised was to Peter (for He who worked effectively in Peter for the apostleship to the circumcised also worked effectively in me toward the Gentiles), and when James, Cephas, and John, who seemed to be pillars, perceived the grace that had been given to me, they gave me and Barnabas the right hand of fellowship, that we should go to the Gentiles and they to the circumcised. They desired only that we should remember the poor, the very thing which I also was eager to do.

Now when Peter had come to Antioch, I withstood him to his face, because he was to be blamed; for before certain men came from James, he would eat with the Gentiles; but when they came, he withdrew and separated himself, fearing those who were of the circumcision.

—GALATIANS 2:1–2, 7–12

The last paragraph of this passage reminds us that leaders do not always agree with each other. The reason Paul opposed Peter openly about his hypocrisy was because the behavior and its impact were in the open. But how could Paul know he had the positional authority to address Peter in such a way, especially because Peter was one of the original twelve apostles? The key is in the middle paragraph. Overall, Peter was a higher authority, but with the Gentiles, Paul was the authority. Paul was the one ultimately responsible for what happened in Antioch. Peter's actions are not recorded, but neither is any mention to indicate an irreparable split between Peter and Paul. As business leaders who seek to follow the Bible's teachings, we must understand and respect authority. It is a boundary that will help us to know when to engage problems properly, as Paul did. It can also help us to respond properly and constructively, as we can infer Peter did. The first step is to understand and respect authority as coming from God. When we start there, it is easy to both submit to and exert proper authority.

Clarify Authority

Live It

- Continually make sure you are clear on where your authority starts—and stops.

- Seek to understand the authority of others with whom you interact (for example, peers, leaders, subordinates), and be quick to recognize the authority in different situations.

- Remember that being "the boss" does not make you the authority in all situations; instead, authority follows roles.

- Readily, and humbly, accept directives that come from someone executing proper authority.

- Recognize that misunderstandings concerning authority may be behind strife and other issues.

See It

While working with a Japanese company, I learned the importance of going beyond titles to discern the real authority in certain business situations. The sponsor of our work was the CFO of the North American subsidiary for the company. He was new to the company and to working for a company based in Japan. One of the executives working directly for this CFO was recently assigned to the States from Japan. Because he was new in his role, people did not know him well. The project we were doing for the CFO was peripheral to the Japanese executive's stated responsibilities, so we were told to keep him informed but not "waste" his time. However, one astute client leader suggested we keep this Japanese executive more directly informed and involved, and we followed her advice.

As we later found out, this executive had more authority than his position implied. As the work progressed, this executive would frequently meet with senior company executives, and it was clear they spoke frequently about the project and its progress. The work was officially the responsibility of the CFO, but in this company, the CFO could have been overridden by a subordinate. Properly discerning this authority—which was not readily apparent—was one of the reasons for the project's ultimate success.

43

LEAD AND SUCCEED

REINFORCE AUTHORITY

This story occurred during Jesus's ministry on the earth. Peter, James, and John were three of the twelve disciples. Moses was a leader, and Elijah a prophet, from much earlier in the history of the Israelite people.

> Now after six days Jesus took Peter, James, and John, and led them up on a high mountain apart by themselves; and He was transfigured before them. His clothes became shining, exceedingly white, like snow, such as no launderer on earth can whiten them. And Elijah appeared to them with Moses, and they were talking with Jesus. Then Peter answered and said to Jesus, "Rabbi, it is good for us to be here; and let us make three tabernacles: one for You, one for Moses, and one for Elijah"—because he did not know what to say, for they were greatly afraid. And a cloud came and overshadowed them; and a voice came out of the cloud, saying, "This is My beloved Son. Hear Him!" Suddenly, when they had looked around, they saw no one anymore, but only Jesus with themselves. Now as they came down from the mountain, He commanded them that they should tell no one the things they had seen, till the Son of Man had risen from the dead.
>
> —MARK 9:2–9

Although He is God, Jesus walked the earth as a man under the Father's authority and in the anointing of the Holy Spirit. If we liken this situation to authority in business, Jesus did not hold the top role, but rather that of a senior executive reporting to the president, CEO, or chairman. Jesus "checked in" with the Father regularly in prayer, and here is an instance where the Father reinforced Jesus as His chosen authority. It is interesting to note this episode is recorded shortly after Peter had openly questioned Jesus about the future suffering and rejection He would soon face. (See Mark 8:31–33.) Only three disciples were present when the Father reinforced Jesus's authority, and Peter was among them. When direction is difficult and people begin to question it, it is important for authority to be reinforced by

44

Clarify Authority

more senior leaders. Questioned authority left unaddressed can divide focus and eventually lead to strife and insubordination. Reinforce the authority of the leaders who work for you, especially at difficult times—and ask your leader to reinforce your authority when it is needed. It is proper and necessary at times, and it does not indicate a weakness.

Live It

• Establish authority for leaders, especially when they are new in their positions, by openly communicating their roles and responsibilities to them and others.

• Advise people to listen to and follow the leaders you have established.

• Be careful not to usurp the authority of others by taking on their responsibilities.

• Be careful not to undermine the authority of others by words or actions that could lead people to question their authority.

• Be visible in showing your support for the authority of others.

• Stay close enough to the "action" to know if you need to reinforce authority.

• Ask your leader to reinforce your authority if it has been challenged or if you feel others may not acknowledge or understand it.

See It

One executive put his consultants in an awkward spot. The aggressive multiyear agreement required the consulting team to bring new concepts and techniques to the company, and the executive wanted to be sure his company would benefit from the consultants' new perspectives and approaches. He repeatedly encouraged the consultants to push for topics they felt strongly about—and press hard on members of his organization and on him personally. He even criticized them for not doing enough pressing over the first few weeks of their relationship.

45

LEAD AND SUCCEED

However, the executive failed to communicate the same message to the leaders of his organization. Resistance was both frequent and intense, even when people had been involved in tailoring the recommendations to the business. At times, the executive sided with those who were resisting even though he had earlier agreed the recommendations were appropriate. The issues negatively impacted the project's results and schedule.

What the executive did not recognize was that the consultants needed a degree of authority to fulfill his high expectations of them—in particular to help push his staff to accept some changes that had eluded them in the past. He wanted substantial change but without difficulty or the need to make significant adjustments, which was not realistic. Minimal progress was achieved at first, and the progress that was made was painful for everyone involved. Eventually, the expectations were clarified and more progress was achieved, but by then, strife was an issue and the project did not fully reach its original potential.

CONSIDER THE NEED FOR SPECIAL AUTHORITY

This situation occurred shortly before Jesus was crucified. In particular, these events preceded Jesus's triumphant entry into Jerusalem on Palm Sunday—the week before the first Easter, or Resurrection, morning.

> Now when they drew near Jerusalem, to Bethphage and Bethany, at the Mount of Olives, He sent two of His disciples; and He said to them, "Go into the village opposite you; and as soon as you have entered it you will find a colt tied, on which no one has sat. Loose it and bring it. And if anyone says to you, 'Why are you doing this?' say, 'The Lord has need of it,' and immediately he will send it here." So they went their way, and found the colt tied by the door outside on the street, and they loosed it. But some of those who stood there said to them, "What are you doing, loosing the colt?" And they spoke to them just as Jesus had commanded. So they let them go.
>
> —MARK 11:1–6

46

Clarify Authority

When you assign special tasks to people who lack the needed authority in their regular positions, it is important for you to establish the authority before they begin the work. In this case, Jesus ensured that those who would question the disciples knew it was the Lord's request they were fulfilling. When you assign special authority, you are extending your authority to others and making it clear the person acts on your behalf. Also, it is very important that the authority message come from the "right" level and person so the message is credible. Carefully consider the needed authority before instructing people to undertake a task to ensure they feel supported rather than "exposed" and uncomfortable. This action will also help to build both willingness and confidence for the work you need them to complete.

Live It

- Consider the person's existing and perceived level of authority; this is especially important if the assignment is temporary.

- Think ahead about how others may react to the assignment.

- Clarify any special authority necessary for the person to effectively and efficiently perform the assigned work— communicating both to that person and to others who need to know about it.

- Meet with the person to discuss how you want the authority to be applied, as well as the potential for any difficult reactions and how best to handle them.

- Check in frequently during the assignment, with attention to ensuring that authority is not a barrier.

- After the assignment, debrief the situation to understand the experience and apply learning to the future.

See It

Early in my career, I worked for a high technology company that filed bankruptcy shortly after I joined as a financial analyst. One of the vital projects necessary to move the company through bankruptcy reorganization

LEAD AND SUCCEED

was to address ongoing payments to the secured creditors where it was difficult to calculate appropriate payments. The company was given a short time from the bankruptcy judge to resolve the problem before the court would impose a difficult and costly resolution. I was asked to look into the problem and propose a workable, ongoing solution.

Interestingly, the resolution was not too difficult. Most of the needed information to do the reconciliation was provided by the customers with their payments. However, the information resided in a different department—one with historically poor relationships with my department. The new leader of my department was wise in her approach. She first made sure the work was openly authorized by the controller, the leader to whom both groups reported. Then she approached the leaders of the other department to describe our planned work and request their assistance. It worked like a charm. Our small team working on the problem was given access and support, and shortly, the problem was resolved—avoiding a costly court stipulation. It would have been much more difficult to meet the tight time frames if our leader had not correctly discerned the actions needed to gain support and give the team the necessary authority to conduct the work.

ESTABLISH AUTHORITY IN A NEW REALITY

This episode happened directly after the great Flood. Noah and his family had just left the ark, and the Lord had promised never to destroy the earth with a flood again.

> So God blessed Noah and his sons, and said to them: "Be fruitful and multiply, and fill the earth. And the fear of you and the dread of you shall be on every beast of the earth, on every bird of the air, on all that move on the earth, and on all the fish of the sea. They are given into your hand. Every moving thing that lives shall be food for you. I have given you all things, even as the green herbs."
>
> —GENESIS 9:1–3

Noah had been the protector of the animals, but now with the Flood over, a new reality emerged. God reestablished Noah and his family (and

48

Clarify Authority

thus the human race) as authority over the animal kingdom, just as He had originally established it under Adam. But God did not assume Noah would understand this—instead, He specifically stated it. During business transformations, many of the expected or historic relationships between groups and people can change—the "who does what" may be dramatically different. But people may not readily recognize the changes, which means they will work by the old rules. When you carefully communicate the new authority and other expectations, you help people understand some of the detailed aspects of the new reality. You also help avoid the common risk where people fail to understand and respect the new authority necessary for the transformation to succeed.

Live It

- Recognize when you are entering changing conditions that may require modifications in authority and boundaries.

- Recognize that others may not even see what you see, so you may need to explain the source of the change.

- Begin by communicating the changes in authority to those who hold that authority, ensuring the changes are clear with them first.

- Communicate to others who need to recognize and respond to those authority changes.

- Monitor whether people are understanding and working in accordance with the authority changes.

- Further communicate to reinforce the new authority, as appropriate.

See It

In one company's major restructuring, a large group of employees moved from one organization to another. The new organization was responsible for day-to-day operations, while the original organization acted as a liaison to the business units the new organization served. Although it was clear the employees were now in a different department, the authority was not adequately clarified, and it was even "muddier" because the people still worked together, just in different capacities.

On a few occasions after the transition, employees who had moved to the new department approached their former leaders. They had concerns and disagreements about the new department's policies and actions. Instead of pointing these employees back to their new leaders or working with those leaders to address the situations, some of the previous leaders took direct action. In doing so, they undermined the authority and made it more difficult for the new leaders to fulfill their charter. Soon some of the leaders between the two groups were in strife, and it took an outside facilitator to work with the teams to restore adequate functioning of both groups. If the new authorities had been better clarified, it is likely this painful and damaging problem could have been avoided.

REST IN GOD'S AUTHORITY SELECTIONS

After leaving Egypt, the Israelites had been wandering in the wilderness for more than one year when this situation occurred. The people were complaining about not having the food they preferred, including meat. After approaching God about the problem, Moses was fulfilling the steps God had told him to do.

> So Moses went out and told the people the words of the LORD, and he gathered the seventy men of the elders of the people and placed them around the tabernacle. Then the LORD came down in the cloud, and spoke to him, and took of the Spirit that was upon him, and placed the same upon the seventy elders; and it happened, when the Spirit rested upon them, that they prophesied, although they never did so again.
>
> But two men had remained in the camp: the name of one was Eldad, and the name of the other Medad. And the Spirit rested upon them. Now they were among those listed, but who had not gone out to the tabernacle; yet they prophesied in the camp. And a young man ran and told Moses, and said, "Eldad and Medad are prophesying in the camp." So

Clarify Authority

Joshua the son of Nun, Moses' assistant, one of his choice men, answered and said, "Moses my lord, forbid them!" Then Moses said to him, "Are you zealous for my sake? Oh, that all the LORD's people were prophets and that the LORD would put His Spirit upon them!" And Moses returned to the camp, both he and the elders of Israel.

—NUMBERS 11:24–30

Moses had to endure the first challenge to his leadership at this point. The selected leaders were told to go to the tent, which was the tabernacle where Moses met directly with God. However, two of the leaders failed to follow the instructions and were taking actions that could have led others to follow them instead of Moses. Notice Moses's response indicated his trust in God. He knew God had selected him to lead the people, and it was His privilege to select others if He wanted to do so. It is important for us to realize, especially as business leaders, that God has retained sovereign control over establishing authorities on the earth, as Romans 13:1 says. Moses clearly understood this, and he rested in the knowledge that God was ultimately in control of the authority he needed. Moses held an awesome leadership responsibility, so if he was able to trust in God's choices, we do well to follow his example.

Live It

- Remember that God is ultimately in control of establishing all authority.

- Be sure you seek to hold positions where God wants you to be rather than ones you desire or have obtained through your own actions; it will give you confidence in difficult times.

- Be prepared for challenges to your authority—and move quickly when they happen.

- Pray when challenges arise and seek God to clarify and/or reconfirm that you are in the right place at the right time; the

LEAD AND SUCCEED

challenge may indicate God wants you to move on, or it may
simply be a challenge you must address.

- Ask God to help you take the needed action, including any
  adjustments to address the immediate issue and avoid similar
  issues in the future.

- Rest in God's selection—it will enable you to portray confidence while you address the issue.

See It

The communications director of a national event-planning company
shook his head as he read a meeting invitation. "Not another meeting with
the executive vice president," he thought. "I sure hope he's in a better mood
this time."

Sadly, that wasn't the case. The executive vice president typically was
pleasant. But he wasn't pleasant at the last meeting—and not again that day.
He went into a lengthy diatribe reprimanding the communications director
yet again for not submitting his budget proposal. "This guy won't let me
get a word in," the communications director thought. "My detailed budget
proposal is sitting right there on this guy's desk. He's even highlighted some
key points. How can he say I haven't submitted it?"

When he got an opportunity to speak, the communications director used
the utmost tact to point to the budget proposal on his desk.

"No it isn't! Write one," the executive vice president barked, and then
dismissed the communications director without further discussion.

Later that day, the CFO dropped by the communication director's office.
The two had been friends for years. "You need to know the executive vice
president has written a memo demanding permission from the CEO to fire
you. He calls you 'the worst disaster in company history,'" the CFO warned
him. "You need to do something."

On the way home that evening, the communications director searched
his heart. He felt he was the right man in the right job and completely at
peace about the wisdom of his budget proposal. The executive vice president's actions seemed nothing short of vindictive, and he couldn't think of
anything he had done to offend him.

52

Clarify Authority

The communications director decided to leave it in God's hands. A month later, the executive vice president's office was empty. The communications director was both sad and relieved. He also was more certain than ever he was right where God wanted him to be.

CONCLUSION

Authority: it is a word that can convey a negative context for various reasons—some valid and others that are inappropriate. However, authority is a vital requirement for a successful business. As a business leader, clarifying and reinforcing proper authority are important aspects of your work. When you handle authority God's way, it is a helpful business tool for you and others to achieve results together.

chapter five

MAKE THE RIGHT DECISIONS
Use faith and wisdom to determine the best choices

M AKING DECISIONS IS an important and never-ending leadership activity. These decisions could be about anything from business direction to solving a problem to determining the appropriate funding for a new project. The Bible contains a number of important principles to help business leaders be most effective and successful in their decision making—principles that get at the heart of the underlying thoughts toward decisions as well as specific actions to enhance them.

DO YOUR OWN RESEARCH
Around 450 B.C., approximately one hundred years after the return of the first Jewish exiles from Babylon, Nehemiah went to Jerusalem. His goal was to rebuild the city walls and gates, which were still in disrepair.

> So I came to Jerusalem and was there three days. Then I arose in the night, I and a few men with me; I told no one what my God had put in my heart to do at Jerusalem; nor was there any animal with me, except the one on which I rode. And I went out by night through the Valley Gate to the Serpent Well and the Refuse Gate, and viewed the walls of Jerusalem which were broken down and its gates which were burned with fire.
>
> —NEHEMIAH 2:11–13

In today's time-pressured business world, it can be easy to make quick decisions based on limited information or to simply rely on the representations of others about what should be done. Nehemiah's example emphasizes

LEAD AND SUCCEED

it is important to build your own in-depth understanding before making some decisions. Nehemiah knew he would face opposition from Israel's enemies in his work to rebuild the wall. Although he knew God was with him (see Nehemiah 1:11–2:6), Nehemiah chose a thoughtful, careful approach to understanding the situation and planning what to do. When making decisions in political or challenging circumstances, few things will serve you better than doing your own research. You will build a deeper understanding than you may even recognize—an understanding that will help you to pray more effectively and perhaps even be more open to God when He instructs you on what to do.

Live It

- Recognize the nature of the situation and how much detailed knowledge you need to be successful.

- Identify the needed information by considering the detailed decisions you must make (for example, where you should start, how much time and resources you need).

- Discern how much you should share with others in the early stages of your decision making and planning; it may be best to keep some information to yourself until you are sure of the decision and its implications.

- Identify the best time and way to do your research, knowing others will observe what you do and try to interpret what it means.

See It

During one complex, multiyear project, I was asked to perform an assessment. Various issues had arisen, from performance failures to interpersonal difficulties. Over the years, I have learned the importance of being personally involved in data collection—even though it is time-consuming—because it builds deeper understanding of the issues and helps me to target my prayers. My original plan was to use a two-person team to conduct two-hour interviews with twelve key leaders. In reviewing and approving the plan,

Make the Right Decisions

one sponsor wanted to go broader and deeper, hearing from more people to convince everyone we had done a thorough job of surfacing the many points of view. So we expanded the interview list from twelve to thirty-five. She was right. Talking with a broader array of people proved helpful in preparing recommendations to address the complex root causes and build relationships needed to move forward. It was clear to everyone we had done a good job of "due diligence." The recommendations were readily accepted and implemented, and they began to produce positive results quickly.

CONSIDER THE INPUT OF OTHERS

Abraham, the patriarch of the nation of Israel, had a close relationship with God. This relationship is best demonstrated when God confided in Abraham concerning His plan to destroy Sodom and Gomorrah. He did not want to hide from Abraham what He was about to do. Abraham did not want God to destroy the cities, knowing his nephew Lot lived there.

And Abraham came near and said, "Would You also destroy the righteous with the wicked? Suppose there were fifty righteous within the city; would You also destroy the place and not spare it for the fifty righteous that were in it? Far be it from You to do such a thing as this, to slay the righteous with the wicked, so that the righteous should be as the wicked; far be it from You! Shall not the Judge of all the earth do right?" So the LORD said, "If I find in Sodom fifty righteous within the city, then I will spare all the place for their sakes." Then Abraham answered and said, "Indeed now, I who am but dust and ashes have taken it upon myself to speak to the Lord: Suppose there were five less than the fifty righteous; would You destroy all of the city for lack of five?" So He said, "If I find there forty-five, I will not destroy it." And he spoke to Him yet again and said, "Suppose there should be forty found there?" So He said, "I will not do it for the sake of forty." Then he said, "Let not the Lord be angry, and I will speak: Suppose thirty should be found there?" So He said, "I will not do it if I find thirty there." And he said,

57

LEAD AND SUCCEED

"Indeed now, I have taken it upon myself to speak to the
Lord: Suppose twenty should be found there?" So He said,
"I will not destroy it for the sake of twenty." Then he said,
"Let not the Lord be angry, and I will speak but once more:
Suppose ten should be found there?" And He said, "I will
not destroy it for the sake of ten." So the LORD went His
way as soon as He had finished speaking with Abraham;
and Abraham returned to his place.

—GENESIS 18:23–33

The sovereign, all-knowing God wasn't lacking the information He needed
to take action with Sodom and Gomorrah. He simply valued his relationship
with Abraham so much that He respected Abraham's thoughts and feelings about the matter. By consulting with Abraham about His decision, God
showed Abraham that respect. In turn, Abraham's faith and trust in God
were built up by God's respect for him.

For us, listening to the advice of others not only shows respect, but it can
also give us necessary details about how to best handle the situation. Their
perspectives will, at the least, impact our understanding and perhaps our
view of the situation. If the additional information causes us to make a wiser
decision, the extra effort is well worth it. But even if it does not change our
planned actions, we can earn additional respect as someone who is open to
others' views, especially if we explain our final decision and include reference to the points of view we gained by listening to others.

Live It

- Remember it is not possible for you to already know everything you need to know when making important decisions.

- Seek advice and counsel from those who are close to the
  situation—and demonstrate you are willing to change your
  plans based on their input.

- Recognize that people with in-depth knowledge may be
  apprehensive to speak candidly, so create an environment that

Make the Right Decisions

helps them to speak freely—both in the immediate situation and in general.

- Gather enough facts and opinions from others before making your decision while balancing this with moving forward in a timely manner.

See It

On one fast-paced project, a member had become negative and disruptive to the effectiveness of the team. Her frequent interruptions were putting the team behind schedule, and many felt the interruptions were not worth the time. Also, the way she spoke about her concerns was causing some hard feelings. The team facilitators planned to openly address future interruptions in a specific way but sought counsel from a key manager first. The manager knew the individual well and understood why the issue needed to be addressed. However, she felt the planned approach ran the risk of being even more disruptive to the team. Instead, the manager and facilitators created a plan to give the individual a role on the team: the role of "inquisitor." In this role, the team member would be expected to raise questions and concerns with the designs and plans, but to do so at specific times so the team had time to explore the ideas before dealing with her concerns. The "inquisitor" would help the team to carefully consider the complexities and avoid making naïve decisions—or repeat problems from the past. The positive and unexpected consequence of implementing the new role was she became more constructive and less negative in how she raised her concerns. The whole team saw the value of her contributions and felt good about the decisions they made together. The project was a success, and this event became a major turning point for the woman and her relationship with others at the company.

HEAR THE WHOLE STORY BEFORE DECIDING

The books of 1 and 2 Timothy were written by the apostle Paul to his protégé, Timothy, as letters of instruction to a pastor. The passage from Proverbs augments Paul's advice to Timothy.

59

LEAD AND SUCCEED

> Do not receive an accusation against an elder except from
> two or three witnesses.
>
> —1 TIMOTHY 5:19

> He who answers a matter before he hears it, it is folly and
> shame to him.
>
> —PROVERBS 18:13

Leaders who take action based on one side of a story risk making poor decisions. They also inadvertently motivate people to run quickly to them for a decision, especially if there are better facts on the other side. Hasty decisions can both negatively impact the immediate situation and lead to problems in team dynamics. As a business leader, you do well to listen to the Bible's advice and consistently examine all sides of a situation. You will benefit from making better decisions and show respect for everyone involved.

Live It

- Be aware of situations that are likely to have multiple sides.

- Hold off reaching conclusions based on your first hearing— everyone will tell their story in the best light possible.

- Ask questions to gain understanding, including what actions have been taken to resolve the issue before bringing it to you.

- Identify others you may want to consult for additional information and perspective.

- Remember to act in a way that reinforces or discourages the way the situation was brought to your attention for the future.

See It

During an especially difficult and understaffed project, a general manager agreed to reassign a member of one subteam to another subteam after hearing only the requester's argument. The general manager's "get it done"

Make the Right Decisions

style was well known within the company, and the reasons seemed right to him based on the story he heard. But the "losing" subteam was furious at the general manager and at the leader of the other subteam who made the request. Whether or not the decision was best could be debated, but it did delay the outputs for the "losing" group and led to hard feelings between people who needed to work together. Most damaging, however, was the perception about the general manager: you did not need to have the best argument when making a request; just get there first to tell your story.

LET PEACE BE YOUR PRIMARY CRITERION

The apostle Paul authored the letter to the Colossians, an early Christian church in Asia Minor. This passage falls within a section of the letter giving instructions on how to live a life pleasing to God.

> And let the peace (soul harmony which comes) from Christ rule (act as umpire continually) in your hearts [deciding and settling with finality all questions that arise in your minds, in that peaceful state] to which as [members of Christ's] one body you were also called [to live]. And be thankful (appreciative), [giving praise to God always].
> —COLOSSIANS 3:15, AMP

Business leaders are often called upon to make decisions with imperfect or incomplete information, or to choose among alternatives that all seem "right." At these times, we need to pray and seek the alternative that gives us peace. God sees ahead and knows the best alternative, so we can rely on Him to give us clear indication of what decision to make. The hardest part can be holding off making a decision until we have peace about one of the alternatives. It can be difficult to withstand the pressure to make an immediate decision when it is not yet clear which decision is best, but we risk making a poor decision if we allow ourselves to be pressured before sensing God's approval. This peace is not necessarily a series of thoughts that come to our mind; rather it is often a sense of calm on the inside when we think about one of the alternatives.

LEAD AND SUCCEED

Live It

- Recognize that you will often be required to decide among several "right" or "not quite right" alternatives or to make decisions with limited information.

- Begin by asking God to help you make a wise decision.

- Research the situation and alternatives carefully to ensure you have a good understanding.

- Prayerfully consider the alternatives one at a time, trying to envision the results of each.

- Sense the degree of peace or discomfort you feel about each alternative.

- Hold off deciding if you find yourself uncomfortable about the alternatives—you may not be considering the right one yet.

- Go with the decision that gives you inner peace, even if it seems like a less-than-optimum choice, because God will direct you to the best choice when you put your trust in Him.

See It

I was admittedly frustrated. In working on one particularly complex client program, we were getting little traction. On the "people" aspects of projects (where I focus my efforts), it is often extremely difficult to make progress without spending time with people, and this was the problem we faced. Everyone we needed to work with was "fighting fires," and even though these leaders agreed that our work was vital to resolving many of the issues they faced, they simply had competing responsibilities they believed were more important. Year-end was approaching, and schedules would be even harder to coordinate. In praying about what to do, I did not feel a peace about our proposed solution: getting the top sponsor to require the people to work with us. In some environments, that answer would have been exactly right, but I could not "get comfortable" with it and asked the team to work with me on another solution.

Make the Right Decisions

In the end, we redirected our efforts to develop a workshop even though it seemed to be of lesser value at the time. The workshop was rolled out early the following year and became an unexpectedly valuable tool in resolving the issues the organization faced—and it was not even considered to be an option until we faced a problem.

AVOID MAKING HASTY DECISIONS

Just as Israel was becoming active in her conquest of the Promised Land, the people ran into trouble. The tribes in Canaan recognized Israel's early successes at Jericho and Ai. Consequently, the Gibeonites sought a treaty with Israel but did so in a deceptive way.

> But when the inhabitants of Gibeon heard what Joshua had done to Jericho and Ai, they worked craftily, and went and pretended to be ambassadors. And they took old sacks on their donkeys, old wineskins torn and mended, old and patched sandals on their feet, and old garments on themselves; and all the bread of their provision was dry and moldy. And they went to Joshua, to the camp at Gilgal, and said to him and to the men of Israel, "We have come from a far country; now therefore, make a covenant with us." Then the men of Israel said to the Hivites, "Perhaps you dwell among us; so how can we make a covenant with you?" But they said to Joshua, "We are your servants." And Joshua said to them, "Who are you, and where do you come from?"
>
> So they said to him: "From a very far country your servants have come, because of the name of the LORD your God; for we have heard of His fame, and all that He did in Egypt, and all that He did to the two kings of the Amorites who were beyond the Jordan—to Sihon king of Heshbon, and Og king of Bashan, who was at Ashtaroth. Therefore our elders and all the inhabitants of our country spoke to us, saying, 'Take provisions with you for the journey, and go to meet them, and say to them, "We are your servants; now therefore, make a covenant with us."' This bread of ours we

63

LEAD AND SUCCEED

took hot for our provision from our houses on the day we departed to come to you. But now look, it is dry and moldy. And these wineskins which we filled were new, and see, they are torn; and these our garments and our sandals have become old because of the very long journey." Then the men of Israel took some of their provisions; but they did not ask counsel of the LORD. So Joshua made peace with them, and made a covenant with them to let them live; and the rulers of the congregation swore to them.

And it happened at the end of three days, after they had made a covenant with them, that they heard that they were their neighbors who dwelt near them. Then the children of Israel journeyed and came to their cities on the third day. Now their cities were Gibeon, Chephirah, Beeroth, and Kirjath Jearim. But the children of Israel did not attack them, because the rulers of the congregation had sworn to them by the LORD God of Israel. And all the congregation complained against the rulers.

—JOSHUA 9:3–18

As business leaders who seek to apply the Bible's wisdom at work, we need to recognize the danger of making important decisions without prayer. In this situation, Israel's leaders looked at the evidence but failed to "ask counsel of the LORD." In making decisions, we need to pray and solicit advice from people who may have insights into the situation. If you dedicate yourself to performing adequate due diligence, including asking God what to do, you are more likely to make better decisions and avoid the significant credibility gap Israel's leaders faced because of their hasty decision.

Live It

* Beware of situations urging you to make hasty decisions; there may be a problem lurking in the urgency itself.

* Recognize your initial perception may be faulty, and there may even be active attempts to bias your perception.

64

Make the Right Decisions

- Ask questions to better understand the situation and gather input from a variety of people.

- Seek God in prayer before all important decisions, no matter how solid the details look.

- Consider delaying your decision for a day or two to see if your initial perception or intuition changes.

See It

While on vacation, the president of a fast-growing media company took a call from an important client. Could the company put the finishing touches on an important new project? The project urgently needed to be finished within four weeks. Since the project sounded similar to one they had done eighteen months earlier, the president said yes, and the two parties agreed on the financial terms. Back in his office the following week, the president discovered the new project wasn't half finished yet and would be much more labor intensive than anything his company had attempted to that point. The president admitted his error to everyone within the company, worked overtime to help finish the project, and—most importantly—implemented new policies to help prevent similar mistakes in the future.

BE OPEN TO CHANGING YOUR MIND

Shortly after the Israelites were delivered from slavery in Egypt, Moses met with God on Mount Sinai to receive the Ten Commandments. Moses was delayed on the mountaintop, so the people sought leadership from Aaron. Unfortunately, his leadership went astray. When God saw the people had turned aside to worship a golden calf, His anger burned, and He told Moses He was going to destroy the Israelites.

> Then Moses pleaded with the LORD his God, and said: "LORD, why does Your wrath burn hot against Your people whom You have brought out of the land of Egypt with great power and with a mighty hand? Why should the Egyptians speak, and say, 'He brought them out to harm them, to kill them in the mountains, and to consume them from the face

LEAD AND SUCCEED

of the earth'? Turn from Your fierce wrath, and relent from
this harm to Your people. Remember Abraham, Isaac, and
Israel, Your servants, to whom You swore by Your own self,
and said to them, 'I will multiply your descendants as the
stars of heaven; and all this land that I have spoken of I give
to your descendants, and they shall inherit it forever.'" So
the LORD relented from the harm which He said He would
do to His people.

—Exodus 32:11–14

This story shows God modeling an expectation He wants us to fulfill as
leaders: being open to changing our minds based on the input of others.
Certainly God knew the end result of this situation and, in fact, was not
surprised by it at all. But we are not perfect in our understanding of the situations we face and the decisions we need to make. If God in His sovereignty
demonstrated openness to Moses's input, we need to be willing to hear other
points of view and to change our minds at times.

Live It

- Adopt a mind-set that allows you to comfortably say, "I think
  this decision is correct, but I may be wrong"; it will help you
  be prepared for times when you need to consider changing a
  previous or committed decision.

- Actively seek and be truly open to input from others who may
  have alternate views.

- Research additional angles, such as the future implications of
  your decision.

- Openly and humbly communicate any appropriate changes
  to your previous decision in a way that lets people know how
  you came to your conclusions; people are likely to better
  understand your decision and appreciate the complexities and
  your candor.

Make the Right Decisions

See It

In a management meeting, a middle manager's two-page proposal to radically change the corporation's radio advertising strategy was dismissed with little discussion. Afterward, one of the vice presidents had second thoughts. Something was nagging at him. Perhaps the previous decision had been too hasty. After all, the proposed changes were radical. To see if there was merit to the proposal, the vice president interviewed the middle manager, did some additional research, and then worked with the middle manager to go back to the management team with a modified proposal. That proposal ultimately won management approval. The new strategy proved four times more effective than any other radio advertising campaign in the corporation's twenty-two year history—benefits that could have been lost had the first hasty decision stuck.

CONCLUSION

Decisions are required of business leaders as an everyday activity. How leaders make the decisions is just as important as what those decisions are—and at times can be even more important. The Bible provides wisdom for decision making—wisdom that will direct you into the best approach for this area so vital to effective business leadership.

chapter six

ACCEPT COUNSEL AND CORRECTION

*Increase your personal effectiveness through
openness and continual learning*

TODAY'S BUSINESS ENVIRONMENT is complex. Leaders need to be ready to deal with a multitude of difficult topics, some of which may be new to all of the people involved. For instance, few people truly understand the nuances of competing globally, know how to employ innovative technologies effectively, or are well versed at managing a mobile, virtual, global workforce—let alone all of them simultaneously. Yet this is what many of us need to navigate. In these challenging times, it is beneficial to turn frequently to prayer and to wise counsel—and to recognize the importance of continual learning. Maintaining the willing attitude of a learner throughout your career will improve the effectiveness of your actions and also help you to stay current with the continual change business brings.

REMEMBER THE IMPORTANCE OF COUNSEL

The following passages come from Proverbs, the book of wisdom. King Solomon is credited with writing these passages that speak to the importance of counsel.

Where there is no counsel, the people fall;
But in the multitude of counselors there is safety.
—PROVERBS 11:14

Without counsel, plans go awry,
But in the multitude of counselors they are established.
—PROVERBS 15:22

LEAD AND SUCCEED

For by wise counsel you will wage your own war,
And in a multitude of counselors there is safety.

—PROVERBS 24:6

Do you see a man wise in his own eyes?
There is more hope for a fool than for him.

—PROVERBS 26:12

These passages state that a leader's openness to counsel greatly impacts his or her success. Leaders who make important decisions without consulting others are running a huge risk—and they are putting their trust in their own knowledge and capabilities, which the Bible refers to as foolish. Ouch! You can get effective counsel from many directions—from peers to people above and below you organizationally, to people in other parts of the company and even outside your company and industry. Wise leaders seek specific counsel from these sources when needed and seek to learn about a broad range of topics on an ongoing basis.

Live It

- Maintain a teachable attitude.

- Remember God is your primary counselor, so seek Him often in prayer and through reading your Bible, where He may "speak" to you by focusing your attention on certain passages.

- Make sure you speak regularly with at least one mentor/counselor.

- Realize you may need different mentors or counselors for different aspects of your business life.

- Seek mentors who are strong in areas important to your success, especially those areas where you need development— and recognize good mentors may be hard on you at times to help you grow.

Accept Counsel and Correction

- Seek ad hoc counsel from people who have more experience or who have different and even contrary perspectives valuable for you to consider.

- Prayerfully consider the advice of counselors and mentors; God will help you know if you should follow it and how to reconcile any conflicting advice.

- Be a mentor to others; as a leader, it is one of your responsibilities, and it is a way to invest in the lives of others and even learn from them.

See It

During one season of my professional life, I was struggling with the feeling I was not receiving adequate recognition for my results, and I must admit my attitude began to show it as the season grew longer and longer—and longer. Mentors have always been important to me, so when my boss suggested I get additional mentoring from one of the "old-timers" in our business, I jumped at the chance.

Norm was well respected and had no less than four decades of experience in the business. During our chats, he suggested I create several different versions of activity reports for different leaders for whom I was working. Frankly, at first this seemed like "busy work" because it would not directly lead to any further results. Instead, it would simply document results I hoped others would readily recognize (and God would give me credit for too). But I followed his advice and was astonished at the difference this small adjustment made. Norm made a number of other suggestions too—all of which were relatively small changes to what I was doing. I tried them all and benefited noticeably.

At the time I began to meet with Norm, I was also speaking regularly with three other executives for mentoring. I could have easily assumed I was getting enough coaching or that adding another mentor would take too much time. However, I would have missed out on this wonderful opportunity for mentoring from someone whose insights contributed to a big turnaround in my career.

LEAD AND SUCCEED

BE A WILLING PROTÉGÉ

The apostle Paul planted a number of churches in the early years of Christianity. Timothy was a spiritual son to Paul and was leading the church at Ephesus when Paul wrote to him.

> These things I write to you, though I hope to come to you shortly; but if I am delayed, I write so that you may know how you ought to conduct yourself in the house of God, which is the church of the living God, the pillar and ground of the truth....Meditate on these things; give yourself entirely to them, that your progress may be evident to all.
> —1 TIMOTHY 3:14–15; 4:15

Throughout 1 Timothy, Paul gives Timothy a number of instructions on ways of prayer, selection of other leaders, and points of heresy. Timothy was in a key leadership role, but Paul still actively mentored him. After achieving a degree of success, some leaders pull back from receiving mentoring, believing they do not need this type of support from others. The best evidence Timothy was a willing protégé is the existence of 1 and 2 Timothy, which are still ministering to us today. Obviously, Timothy considered this mentoring to be precious to him because he retained these letters and shared them with others.

Live It

- Recognize there will always be people to learn from no matter the success and height of your career—and learning from others may actually become more important as your responsibilities expand.

- Agree to a "contract" with your mentor.
  - How often will you meet or speak with one another?
  - What topics will you cover?
  - How open will your communications be?

72

Accept Counsel and Correction

- Keep your mentor apprised of important events and issues going on in your life.

- Prepare yourself before your mentoring sessions by reviewing notes of your last discussion and thinking through questions, topics, and concerns you would like to discuss.

- Maintain an open attitude toward receiving difficult or touchy messages; a good mentor will care more about your success than your feelings or comfort.

- If the conversations with your mentor do not press and challenge you, seek a new or additional mentor.

See It

"Ouch, that hurt," thought the middle manager during a meeting with her new mentor. Feeling her career was stagnating and her long-time mentor might not be helping enough, the middle manager had reached out to an additional mentor.

This senior executive had a "no-nonsense" communication style, so after listening to her career challenges for about ten minutes, the executive offered his point of view. "It's your attitude that's holding you back. You see yourself as a victim of the unfortunate things that have happened to you. But guess what? We all have those kinds of challenges. What you choose to do with them makes all the difference. You've just chosen to have a bad attitude, and it won't help you."

Although the words stung, the leader instantly knew she had selected a good mentor. Over the next year, the leader met with her mentor regularly, planned meeting topics and questions carefully, and followed his advice. He was right. She had allowed her thinking to become a problem, and unfortunately, her other mentor was not willing to confront her about it. Although she kept both mentoring relationships, she found the advice from her new mentor was providing more results. Soon she felt—and saw—her career aspirations were back on track. Her attitude was restored, and she once again felt satisfied with her career and her work.

BEWARE—SOME COUNSEL MAY BE UNWISE

Jeroboam was one of King Solomon's officials. Jeroboam had received a prophecy stating he would later lead ten of the tribes of Israel, which led him to rebel against Solomon and flee to Egypt to avoid Solomon's attempts to kill him. After Solomon's death, Rehoboam ruled in his place as Israel's fourth king, and Jeroboam returned from Egypt. Jeroboam gathered the Israelites together, and they came to speak to Rehoboam, asking him to lighten the burden of service Solomon had put on them. Rehoboam asked them to return in three days for an answer, so he could seek advice.

Then King Rehoboam consulted the elders who stood before his father Solomon while he still lived, and he said, "How do you advise me to answer these people?" And they spoke to him, saying, "If you will be a servant to these people today, and serve them, and answer them, and speak good words to them, then they will be your servants forever." But he rejected the advice which the elders had given him, and consulted the young men who had grown up with him, who stood before him. And he said to them, "What advice do you give? How should we answer this people who have spoken to me, saying, 'Lighten the yoke which your father put on us'?" Then the young men who had grown up with him spoke to him, saying, "Thus you should speak to this people who have spoken to you, saying, 'Your father made our yoke heavy, but you make it lighter on us'—thus you shall say to them: 'My little finger shall be thicker than my father's waist! And now, whereas my father put a heavy yoke on you, I will add to your yoke; my father chastised you with whips, but I will chastise you with scourges!'"

So Jeroboam and all the people came to Rehoboam the third day, as the king had directed, saying, "Come back to me the third day." Then the king answered the people roughly, and rejected the advice which the elders had given him; and he spoke to them according to the advice of the

Accept Counsel and Correction

young men, saying, "My father made your yoke heavy, but I
will add to your yoke; my father chastised you with whips,
but I will chastise you with scourges!"

—1 Kings 12:6–14

You can read about the full consequences of Rehoboam's decision in the rest of 1 Kings 12.

Rehoboam started with the right action of seeking multiple counselors, but he made a poor decision because he did not choose the best counselors. The consequences were devastating because the people eventually chose to follow another leader, and the kingdom of Israel was severed in two. When a leader follows poor counsel in today's business settings, it may devastate the entire company, although it is more likely to erode business results through issues such as high turnover, low productivity, and low employee morale. Rehoboam appeared to think the people had no other option but to live with his answer. Leaders who hold that kind of thinking typically find people *do* have options and will exercise those options and express their feelings. Select your counselors carefully, and when you receive conflicting advice, be sure to seek God in prayer to resolve the conflict.

Live It

- For especially important decisions, consult several people to get their ideas and recommendations; it will increase your chances of recognizing poor advice.

- Give your counselors as much information as you can share about the situation because the best decisions are ones that fit the full context and are made with an understanding of the implications.

- Give people time to consider their answers; "soak time" often brings new insights into view.

- Be alert to conflicting counsel; it may intentionally or unin-tentionally work to get you off course with God's will.

LEAD AND SUCCEED

- Consider whether you should test the conflicting ideas with your various counselors by asking them what would happen if you followed the other advice—and watch their demeanor while listening to the answer because it can give you additional insights.

- Always—and throughout—seek God in prayer about the counsel you have received, and delay taking action or making the decision until you feel an inner peace about what you are to do.

See It

Despite advice against the decision, an executive promoted a savvy but difficult person to a senior manager position. He would now be responsible for a department of professional services personnel with a good track record for sales and delivery. The executive knew the new senior manager had a reputation for various "people" issues but felt he was a key to enhancing the group's sales performance because of his superior sales track record. Even with direct expressions of concern from some in the department and input from others who knew him, the executive did not understand the extent to which the new senior manager was disliked by those he would now lead. He felt they would simply accept the decision and "live with it."

Dashing even the most moderate of hopes, the new senior manager proved to be even more difficult as a manager than he was as a peer. In a very short period of time, the people on the team "voted with their feet" and left the group—in some cases, opting for lesser positions and positions outside the company to simply get away from him. Eventually, the senior manager was removed and, in response, left the company. But the damage was already done. By failing to act on the counsel people had willingly offered, the executive not only failed in his attempts to enhance the group's performance, but he also lost the team—one that was collaborative and effective. The end result was significantly lowered business performance that reflected poorly on his leadership capabilities.

76

Accept Counsel and Correction

GET ADVICE FROM *THE* SOURCE

This episode happened after David was anointed as king but before he took his role as king. Saul, the king who had been rejected by God, was still in leadership over Israel. David was on the run from Saul to protect his own life.

Then they told David, saying, "Look, the Philistines are fighting against Keilah, and they are robbing the threshing floors." Therefore David inquired of the Lord, saying, "Shall I go and attack these Philistines?" And the Lord said to David, "Go and attack the Philistines, and save Keilah." But David's men said to him, "Look, we are afraid here in Judah. How much more then if we go to Keilah against the armies of the Philistines?" Then David inquired of the Lord once again. And the Lord answered him and said, "Arise, go down to Keilah. For I will deliver the Philistines into your hand." And David and his men went to Keilah and fought with the Philistines, struck them with a mighty blow, and took away their livestock. So David saved the inhabitants of Keilah.

Now it happened, when Abiathar the son of Ahimelech fled to David at Keilah, that he went down with an ephod in his hand. And Saul was told that David had gone to Keilah. So Saul said, "God has delivered him into my hand, for he has shut himself in by entering a town that has gates and bars." Then Saul called all the people together for war, to go down to Keilah to besiege David and his men.

When David knew that Saul plotted evil against him, he said to Abiathar the priest, "Bring the ephod here." Then David said, "O Lord God of Israel, Your servant has certainly heard that Saul seeks to come to Keilah to destroy the city for my sake. Will the men of Keilah deliver me into his hand? Will Saul come down, as Your servant has heard? O Lord God of Israel, I pray, tell Your servant." And the Lord said, "He will come down." Then David said, "Will

77

LEAD AND SUCCEED

the men of Keilah deliver me and my men into the hand of
Saul?" And the LORD said, "They will deliver you." So David
and his men, about six hundred, arose and departed from
Keilah and went wherever they could go. Then it was told
Saul that David had escaped from Keilah; so he halted the
expedition.

—1 SAMUEL 23:1–13

Notice David sought God before he took action that may have seemed
obvious to take. As leaders, we must continually seek God's guidance on
key decisions—and we should not be reticent to seek His guidance multiple
times if the answer is unclear or uncertain for any reason. In David's case,
he received clear direction from God but needed confirmation when the
people raised concerns about going against the Philistines. And when Saul
was coming against him, David sought God again. David knew he had been
anointed as king, but he didn't know how or when God would give him the
kingdom. He also knew Saul hated him and sought to kill him, which were
the immediate issues he obviously needed to "get right." Continually seeking
God at these times gave David the confidence he needed to ensure he was
fulfilling God's specific will in each instance—protecting and preparing him
for his destiny.

Live It

- Remember human counselors can be helpful, but God is the
  source of all true wisdom—as well as an understanding of the
  future.

- Seek God regularly in prayer and Bible reading, and not just
  when you have a problem or critical decision to make; it will
  give you confidence to approach Him even multiple times on
  the same topic if necessary.

- Communicate your plans and be open to the counsel and
  concerns of others, and to adjust your plans based on what
  they say.

Accept Counsel and Correction

- If what you hear causes you to question your plans, do not blindly move forward; instead, seek God again to confirm what to do, knowing He is always open to hearing from you!

- Remember God's will has both a "what" and a "when" to it—and the right answer at the wrong time is wrong.

See It

To me, changing employers has always been a difficult decision. At one point in my career, I found myself at a crossroads. I could continue at my current company, where my career appeared to be on track, or take an opportunity to join a company that was in the early stages of building a capability I wanted to help build. I prayed and felt a peace about the move. But when I announced my plans, a number of people gave me opinions and input that the move would be disastrous for my career. I have to admit their concerns seemed valid based on what I knew about the company. So I sought God again and asked Him to make it so clear I could not miss His plan for me, and I promised to be open to whatever decision that would be. To make a complicated story short, I received confirmation after confirmation I should make the move, and I felt a peace about it, so I accepted the offer. It was a pivotal decision in my career—and one that came with a number of unexpected benefits and challenges. The peace I sought when I received conflicting advice kept me stable in my decision and helped me through the challenges because I knew it was God's chosen path for me.

READILY RECEIVE CORRECTION FROM TRUSTED SOURCES

Approximately nine months before this account, King David committed adultery with Bathsheba. When she became pregnant, David made arrangements to have her husband killed in battle so he could marry her in an attempt to cover his sin. Nathan was the prophet in Israel at the time and was David's confidant and counselor.

> Then the Lord sent Nathan to David. And he came to him, and said to him: "There were two men in one city, one rich and the other poor. The rich man had exceedingly many

79

LEAD AND SUCCEED

flocks and herds. But the poor man had nothing, except one little ewe lamb which he had bought and nourished; and it grew up together with him and with his children. It ate of his own food and drank from his own cup and lay in his bosom; and it was like a daughter to him. And a traveler came to the rich man, who refused to take from his own flock and from his own herd to prepare one for the wayfaring man who had come to him; but he took the poor man's lamb and prepared it for the man who had come to him." So David's anger was greatly aroused against the man, and he said to Nathan, "As the LORD lives, the man who has done this shall surely die! And he shall restore fourfold for the lamb, because he did this thing and because he had no pity."

Then Nathan said to David, "You are the man! Thus says the LORD God of Israel: 'I anointed you king over Israel, and I delivered you from the hand of Saul. I gave you your master's house and your master's wives into your keeping, and gave you the house of Israel and Judah. And if that had been too little, I also would have given you much more! Why have you despised the commandment of the LORD, to do evil in His sight? You have killed Uriah the Hittite with the sword; you have taken his wife to be your wife, and have killed him with the sword of the people of Ammon. Now therefore, the sword shall never depart from your house, because you have despised Me, and have taken the wife of Uriah the Hittite to be your wife.'"

—2 SAMUEL 12:1–10

Nathan did not wait for David to ask for counsel but proactively spoke to him when he saw the problem. He delivered the tough message David needed to hear and was undoubtedly difficult to deliver. David admitted his sin and accepted the consequences.

The most effective mentors are ones who will tell you what you need to know even when you may not want to hear it. Achieving this level of relationship with one or two people should be one of your professional goals.

Accept Counsel and Correction

When you seek counsel, focus on building open and trusting relationships that go both directions—where you can tell them what is on your mind and where they can approach you about issues you have not brought up. This type of counsel will challenge you at times but will be instrumental in your growth as a leader.

Live It

- Maintain an attitude that allows you to readily receive correction without becoming defensive or depressed; you aren't perfect, but neither is anyone else!

- Remember you are likely to need the correction even if it is unexpected, especially if it is coming from a trusted source.

- Use the "catcher's mitt" approach to receiving difficult correction: "catch" the message in an imaginary mitt in front of you, and examine it objectively and unemotionally before deciding if and how to apply it to your life.

- Set aside time to prayerfully consider the correction and other input you have received; God will help you to know what is most relevant and what changes you need to make.

- Identify actions to enhance your capabilities, build on your strengths, and address your shortcomings, starting with the ideas your counselor may have for you.

- Openly admit your mistakes to those who have seen them; it will enhance your credibility.

- Constructively accept any consequences for your mistakes; you will be modeling what you expect from others when you need to correct them.

See It

Fairly early in my career, I found myself in an awkward position. I had accepted a job offer from a competitor, and my leadership team wanted to counter so I would stay. My decision to move was very well thought out—and

LEAD AND SUCCEED

prayerfully considered. There was a certain type of work I wanted to do, and my current firm was not doing it. I consulted with an expert in the field, and he told me about two competitors doing the work. My passion for the field was so strong that I reached out to one of the competitors, and when the offer came, I jumped at the chance.

When my senior leader asked why I was leaving and what it would take for me to stay, I immediately told him what I wanted to do and why. Essentially I closed the door to even considering his offer. It was a truthful response but unwise. As a confidant later told me, "In this business, you never know when your paths will cross again. Even if you knew you wouldn't accept his offer, you should have appeared to be open to it." I didn't ask for advice—I didn't even know I needed it. But I never forgot it. I hadn't realized my desire to be open and honest, along with my strong passion for the work, led me to unintentionally offend a senior leader.

CONCLUSION

You are not perfect—but neither is anyone else. The way you gain advantage in this imperfect world is to continually grow and develop, recognizing that learning is a lifelong requirement and privilege. Leaders who are teachable find themselves in the best position to bring results to their company and grow in their careers. The Bible acknowledges this and shows the importance of ongoing counsel for success.

82

chapter seven

UNDERSTAND COMMITMENT AND MOTIVATION

Discover the keys to gain willing action from others

L EADERSHIP, BY ITS very nature, involves other people. Leaders are called to set direction and help others achieve targeted business results. Since most business results are achieved through the efforts of others, leaders have only indirect influence over achieving them. Leaders who think they can actually control others are sorely mistaken. Yes, strong coercive methods can gain immediate response from others, but God has given mankind a free will to respond, and this is where the coercive approach often proves ineffective in the long run. For these reasons, commitment is vital in business, and leaders who leverage it enhance business results and the effectiveness of their teams. To create a business environment that promotes others to take willing action, you need a deep understanding of commitment and motivation. This chapter provides that foundation, and chapter 8 builds on it by describing specific actions to take.

GET THE "WILL" IN FRONT OF THE "DO"

The apostle Paul authored a letter to the Philippians. He wrote it while in prison, most likely in Rome. Paul established the church in Philippi—a church predominantly of non-Jewish believers.

> Therefore, my beloved, as you have always obeyed, not as in my presence only, but now much more in my absence, work out your own salvation with fear and trembling; for it is God who works in you both to will and to do for His good pleasure. Do all things without complaining and disputing,

LEAD AND SUCCEED

> that you may become blameless and harmless, children of
> God without fault in the midst of a crooked and perverse
> generation, among whom you shine as lights in the world,
> holding fast the word of life, so that I may rejoice in the day
> of Christ that I have not run in vain or labored in vain.
> —PHILIPPIANS 2:12–16

This scripture reflects an important truth about leading people: it is not enough to simply get them to do what is needed. It is also important that their motives line up for best results. Notice the passage mentions "to will" before it mentions "to do." In other words, commitment to do what is right and necessary is essential. This is especially true during the leader's absence—an increasingly common situation in today's virtual, mobile business world. Commitment is also a foundation for a good attitude. One key to gaining this type of commitment is identified in the opening sentence: people need to "own" their portion of the vision and have a reason for doing it. In this case, Paul refers to Christians and their "own salvation"—to gaining benefits from God's kingdom both for eternity and for living life on Earth. In business, the "what's in it for me" may be more difficult to define, but it is necessary for building commitment. Once you clarify those benefits—and others begin to "own" those reasons—the motives naturally drive the right actions and right attitude. Also, you can be confident people will do what they should whether you are present or not, and you can (and should) trust them increasingly. Start with helping people to "will" before they "do," and you'll be well on your way to building the genuine commitment that is an effective foundation for ongoing business results.

Live It

- Explore the reasons people work for your company, in that profession, and on that team; it will help you to identify what is especially motivating to them.

- Ensure people have a clear understanding of why working for you and your company is a wonderful opportunity (and make sure it is a wonderful opportunity).

Understand Commitment and Motivation

- Explore previous situations where people have done what you desire them to do now, and compare these positive examples to current conditions:
  - What were the dynamics of the situation?
  - What were the specific motivators that compelled people to want to work that way?
  - What results were achieved?
  - What benefits were gained for all involved?

- Recognize money is important—particularly in some professions, such as sales—but other factors are also important and may actually be more motivating and tied to long-term commitment.

- Identify areas to use as motivators and avenues for commitment; for example:
  - A "fun and friendly" working environment
  - Working with the "best and brightest"
  - Opportunities to learn and grow new skills and advance in a profession
  - Visibility and recognition inside and outside the group
  - Life-work balance

- Dedicate yourself to creating a work environment that is motivating to the team you want to keep or create, and to laying a strong foundation for long-term commitment.

See It

Early one year, the leadership team for a large department with a difficult charter met to plan their year. I had been working with these leaders for a few months to help them address various "people" issues, so they invited me to attend. One of the goals mentioned by several of the top leaders was to improve "work-life balance" for everyone that year. Heads began to nod, and several people expressed how challenging the previous year had been and how morale was low and people were burned out.

I often used provocative questions to stir conversation with the team, and

LEAD AND SUCCEED

I couldn't resist this opportunity. What would happen if the leaders were to shift their thinking slightly to "life-work balance"? Also, how much fun were people having at work? At first, it seemed no one was going to pick up on my questions, but then one of the leaders rose up and admitted, "You know, even if I were doing this for only eight hours a day, I would still hate it." The leader's own admission led the team to recognize they faced issues beyond simply being out of balance, and they began to discuss what to do to make the environment less taxing and more enjoyable for everyone. They identified a number of adjustments, starting with frequent expressions of appreciation and opportunities to celebrate the small "wins." That year, the leadership team made great progress in building a more motivating work environment, and everyone noticed the difference.

BUILD MOTIVATION GOD'S WAY

The following scriptures relate to the time of King Saul, shortly after he was proclaimed Israel's first king (ending an extended period of time when Israel was ruled by a series of judges). The first passage shows Saul's approach to building commitment. It is an interesting contrast to the second passage, which is God's approach given through the prophet Samuel during Saul's coronation as king.

And Nahash the Ammonite went up and besieged Jabesh-gilead; and all the men of Jabesh said to Nahash, Make a treaty with us, and we will serve you. But Nahash the Ammonite told them, On this condition I will make a treaty with you, that I thrust out all your right eyes and thus lay disgrace on all Israel.

The elders of Jabesh said to Nahash, Give us seven days' time, that we may send messengers through all the territory of Israel. Then, if there is no man to save us, we will come out to you.

Then messengers came to Gibeah of Saul and told the news in the ears of the people; and all the people wept aloud. Now Saul came out of the field after the oxen, and [he] said, What ails the people that they are weeping? And

86

Understand Commitment and Motivation

they told him the words of the men of Jabesh. The Spirit of God came mightily upon Saul when he heard those tidings, and his anger was greatly kindled. And he took a yoke of oxen and cut them in pieces and sent them throughout all the territory of Israel by the hands of messengers, saying, Whoever does not come forth after Saul and Samuel, so shall it be done to his oxen! And terror from the Lord fell on the people, and they came out with one consent.
—1 SAMUEL 11:1–7, AMP

If you will revere and fear the Lord and serve Him and hearken to His voice and not rebel against His commandment, and if both you and your king will follow the Lord your God, it will be good! But if you will not hearken to the Lord's voice, but rebel against His commandment, then the hand of the Lord will be against you, as it was against your fathers.
—1 SAMUEL 12:14–15, AMP

In the second scripture, God balances His message for both positive and negative consequences, answering, "What will I gain by doing this, and what will happen if I don't do it?" in that order. Contrast this balanced message with Saul's one-sided message. It is easy to recognize the one-sided message will only get people to do enough to keep out of trouble, whereas the balanced message builds a foundation for committed action. The command-and-control style of management can gain results, but usually at the expense of true commitment and loyalty. It can also lead people to blindly follow orders, even when they know those actions will cause problems.

History tells of business failures based on problems known to employees and others, yet unrevealed. Of course, there are many leadership failures associated with such problems, and there also may be a history of using strong and coercive leadership to control people's actions. Follow God's more effective approach, and consistently balance your messages. It will help to build genuine commitment to achieving the business results you seek.

LEAD AND SUCCEED

Live It

- Identify the actions you want people to take.

- Consider the natural motivations:
    - Are people naturally drawn to, or away from, taking the desired actions?
    - Are there good reasons for people not to take the desired action?
    - Is there history to consider?

- Identify the positive and negative consequences within your authority and ability to execute.
    - Positive consequences include open appreciation and recognition, small or large monetary rewards, promotions, opportunities for increased responsibility and advancement, and access to important people and information.
    - Negative consequences include withholding any of the above positive consequences as well as increased supervision, reduced authority, negative financial impacts, and disciplinary actions.

- Develop a balanced message that focuses attention on what you want and why, communicates what is to be gained, and directly or indirectly warns people of the potential negative consequences of not following through.

See It

"We need your very best. This is going to be a touchy project—lots of work and little time to get it done. And we've got to get this right. Our company's future is riding on our work here. Everyone is counting on us. Thank you for throwing yourselves completely into this work." With that, the sponsor for an enterprise-wide project concluded his remarks at the project kickoff. The project's goal was extremely ambitious—both in what it targeted to achieve and in the schedule allowed to get the work done.

88

Understand Commitment and Motivation

The handpicked "best and brightest" team was very motivated, but they also knew members of prior projects who were not well rewarded for their extra efforts.

The sponsor took some of the right actions—in particular with the project's leadership team. He gave them exposure to the company's senior executives and to key meetings to propel their careers. But he neglected to take specific action to motivate and reward the rest of the team. The team initially benefitted from being "in the know" about important upcoming company changes, but once the changes were announced, that benefit faded. Before the project was completed, some of the team members had returned to their regular jobs. They did not see the benefit from working so hard and were worried about how the "absence" from their regular jobs could impact their performance ratings. Others stayed but admitted to one another their initial enthusiasm had cooled. They were not sure their efforts were going to be as valuable as they had originally hoped—for the company or for their own career aspirations. The sponsor got part of it right: he focused on motivating the project's top team. But he did not work with those leaders to carry it into the full team. Thus they lost the chance to get the best from a team they worked so hard to select.

DETERMINE WHETHER A PUSH OR PULL STRATEGY IS BEST

The apostle Paul wrote this letter to the Romans approximately twenty-five years after Jesus was crucified and resurrected. The church in Rome was composed primarily of non-Jewish believers, but there was a Jewish minority in the church.

> Or are you [so blind as to] trifle with and presume upon and despise and underestimate the wealth of His kindness and forbearance and long-suffering patience? Are you unmindful or actually ignorant [of the fact] that God's kindness is intended to lead you to repent (to change your mind and inner man to accept God's will)?
>
> —ROMANS 2:4, AMP

LEAD AND SUCCEED

In contrast to other religions—and even to how some view Christianity —God seeks to draw people to Himself with His goodness rather than force us to fulfill His expectation to stay out of hell. The contrast between these two options is a good example of the difference between "pull" and "push" strategies—or what may also be called commitment and compliance. Although some degree of commitment is always necessary in business, compliance is also a viable approach to certain business requirements, and effective leaders are good at determining which strategy is best.

In essence, "pull" strategies are ones based on persuading others—drawing them to act in ways that are desirable. Notice God's desire is to lead people to repentance, and He doesn't choose to push that on us. Instead, He uses His goodness to draw people into it. "Pull" strategies are best when people need to genuinely believe in what they are doing and when fulfilling specific actions is not enough. Repentance is a perfect example for a "pull" strategy because it is a heart issue and not simply an issue of the actions taken. In business, customer satisfaction is an example where people need to be genuinely committed and willing to do what is necessary, and even go "above and beyond" at times.

"Push" strategies are effective in areas where the stakes are not as high and where simply performing the right action is enough. A good business example is handling administrative requirements such as completing expense reports. It is not necessary for people to be committed to the process and system used by the company, but rather to comply with the steps in a timely and accurate manner. Notice the expense report example also comes with a natural "maintenance mechanism": if you do not follow the rules, you will not be reimbursed.

Where leaders often get into trouble is using compliance or "push" strategies when commitment is needed. When this happens, people will typically do what is necessary to stay out of trouble—and no more. When you need more than the minimum, you need a "pull" strategy that leads people to understand both what you want them to do and why. It may sound complicated, but once you understand the difference, you'll find getting what you want from people comes more easily and naturally.

Understand Commitment and Motivation

Live It

• Identify the actions you want people to take.

• Assess the natural motivators and barriers.

  • Are people naturally drawn to take this action? If not, why not?

  • Is this a new action or something people have done to some extent in the past?

  • What are the benefits on all levels if these actions are taken? To the customers? To the company? To the business unit? To the department? To the individuals?

• Assess whether it is important for people to take action because they think it is the right thing to do, or if it is adequate for people to simply perform the expectations— recognizing it is easy to assume the action itself will be enough when it may not be.

• Identify whether a "pull" or "push" strategy is best—and recognize that a combination may be needed for projects and other complex situations (i.e., "pull" for some components or jobs, and "push" for others).

• Research and plan the implementation of your strategy.

  • For push commitment, it is important to communicate:

    • What is expected

    • The timing, frequency, and other details

    • The consequences for not complying in a timely manner

  • For pull commitment, it is important to communicate:

    • What is expected

    • The timing, frequency, and other details

    • Why the expectations are important

  • Benefits to everyone involved, with particular emphasis on benefits to individuals

LEAD AND SUCCEED

- Positive consequences for performing as expected
- Negative consequences for not performing as expected, with emphasis on what people will naturally lose if they do not perform rather than punishments for not performing—a key difference between "pull" and "push" strategies

- Establish mechanisms to monitor the needed actions, which need to be permanent for "push" strategies (remember the expense report example) and temporary for "pull" strategies, until people believe in what they are doing and naturally work to fulfill the expectations.

See It

One service provider needed to make dramatic changes to its operational model to increase productivity and reduce costs. A field dispatch process was at the core of the new operating vision. Rather than handling service calls by territory, the dispatch system and process would smooth the workload and improve consistency of response times. The process was a radical change from current operations, so the project team decided to run a live pilot in Florida, and they brought me in to evaluate it and prepare the plan for nationwide rollout.

A key element in planning for a successful implementation is to determine the ultimate way the change will be sustained over time, and pull/push strategies are a key part of that. Because commitment takes longer to achieve, I recommend companies build it where it will provide the most benefit. If compliance will be effective enough, it can be a better option in many cases.

At first, it seemed a compliance strategy would be adequate. Why should the technicians care about the source of their calls? But as I explored the nature of the change, I found otherwise. The technicians had developed routines, such as informal call trading to build skills and coordinating lunch schedules to share news and learning. The routines would be significantly disrupted by the dispatch process. The project team was aware of the resistance but felt the issues would be resolved quickly once the new process was implemented. We did a formal assessment that warned strongly about the need to adjust to the dispatch process, so we met with some of the techni-

92

cians in the pilot. How could we gain the benefits from the dispatch process without losing the flexibility they felt was necessary for their jobs?

In the end, the process was altered to allow technicians to trade calls and coordinate lunch and parts runs so they could maintain relationships and continue to mentor each other. These were among the commitment elements for the new dispatch process. When the changes were rolled out across the country, the fact the Florida technicians designed parts of the process was highlighted to give the changes more credibility. The changes were quickly and successfully rolled out, and the combination pull/push strategy was instrumental in helping people accept the new operational model.

DECIDE WHETHER BROAD COMMITMENT IS WARRANTED

In this story, King David works to bring the ark of the covenant—the visible representation of God's presence—into Jerusalem. Notice how David actively solicits broad involvement across Israel in bringing the ark into Jerusalem, which was important for raising the funds necessary to achieve his ultimate goal of building the temple.

> Then David consulted with the captains of thousands and hundreds, and with every leader. And David said to all the assembly of Israel, "If it seems good to you, and if it is of the LORD our God, let us send out to our brethren everywhere who are left in all the land of Israel, and with them to the priests and Levites who are in their cities and their common-lands, that they may gather together to us; and let us bring the ark of our God back to us, for we have not inquired at it since the days of Saul." Then all the assembly said that they would do so, for the thing was right in the eyes of all the people.
>
> —1 CHRONICLES 13:1–4

> Then the leaders of the fathers' houses, leaders of the tribes of Israel, the captains of thousands and of hundreds, with the officers over the king's work, offered willingly. They gave

LEAD AND SUCCEED

for the work of the house of God five thousand talents and ten thousand darics of gold, ten thousand talents of silver, eighteen thousand talents of bronze, and one hundred thousand talents of iron. And whoever had precious stones gave them to the treasury of the house of the LORD, into the hand of Jehiel the Gershonite. Then the people rejoiced, for they had offered willingly, because with a loyal heart they had offered willingly to the LORD; and King David also rejoiced greatly.

—1 CHRONICLES 29:6–9

Read 1 Chronicles 13 and 15 to see the full story of how David brought the ark to Jerusalem and how he faced an unexpected problem where broad-based commitment undoubtedly helped him in the long run.

David was the king—the highest authority in Israel. Yet on the point of bringing the ark into Jerusalem, he did not force his desires and instead worked to build broad commitment among the people. David wanted them to agree with his decision because it was a major step in his overall goal of building the temple—and he needed their willingness to fund the project. Business projects often suffer from a lack of commitment, which frequently comes from a leader's unilateral decision forced on others with little explanation or attempts to help others buy into the project. David, however, recognized the nature of his project and how he truly needed people to willingly work with him on it. He also rightly understood exerting his authority might be counterproductive. In business, you may need to launch difficult efforts where you need others to believe it is the right thing to do and not simply take action because they are being forced to do it. Thinking about the long-term requirements will help you discern where you need to build broad commitment. When it is necessary for success, dedicate yourself to the extra investment up front because it will bring a valuable return.

Live It

- Develop a vision for what you are working to achieve, and consider how you want and need people to participate in it.

94

Understand Commitment and Motivation

- Analyze the need for commitment by each group of people impacted and for specific components of your vision. For example:
  - You may need executive commitment to every element of the vision and need to work actively, in the beginning, to achieve it.
  - For some minor system changes, you may need only compliance because it is easy to ensure people are taking the needed actions.
  - For process changes, you may need commitment because people can easily work around your new process, and commitment is a way to help ensure the process will be followed.
- Where you need to build broad-based commitment, work with others—many others—to tailor elements of the approach to the people, their environment, and their preferences.

See It

"We're not making progress in these workshops. It's time to regroup and change our approach." Our team's project schedule was starting to slip, and I was concerned we were on a path where the schedule problem could become even worse. Our client had a strong consensus culture, and our first two workshops had been "wasted" while participants scrutinized the approach we were using. They asked many questions—some repeatedly—and offered minor suggestions on a proven approach we knew would be successful. We needed to honor the client's culture of involvement yet focus attention where it would be useful—on the decisions necessary for the success of the project. Unfortunately, our first two meetings had established an expectation we now needed to redirect.

We decided to pull people into the content—and away from the approach itself—with a data collection activity. We went about gathering individual input on the topics for the workshop. When the next workshop started, we began by immediately showing the data collected, which pulled the client's team into valuable discussion. We had lost time with our rocky start but

95

LEAD AND SUCCEED

managed to recover the schedule with some extra work. Had I thought through the needed commitment by group and component, I would have dispensed with a detailed explanation of the approach and opted for moving into the workshop content more quickly. I knew the client was oriented toward consensus, and my detailed explanation on the approach actually triggered them to comment and suggest changes—a problem I could have easily avoided with the right planning.

GUARD AGAINST HARSHNESS

Many times during the reigns of Saul and David, the Israelites were at war with the Philistines. Just before this particular situation, Jonathan, King Saul's son, had attacked and killed approximately twenty Philistines with only the help of his armor bearer. (See 1 Samuel 14:14.) While Jonathan was gone, Saul uttered a harsh directive that led to this problem.

> And the men of Israel were distressed that day, for Saul had placed the people under oath, saying, "Cursed is the man who eats any food until evening, before I have taken vengeance on my enemies." So none of the people tasted food. Now all the people of the land came to a forest; and there was honey on the ground. And when the people had come into the woods, there was the honey, dripping; but no one put his hand to his mouth, for the people feared the oath. But Jonathan had not heard his father charge the people with the oath; therefore he stretched out the end of the rod that was in his hand and dipped it in a honeycomb, and put his hand to his mouth; and his countenance brightened. Then one of the people said, "Your father strictly charged the people with an oath, saying, 'Cursed is the man who eats food this day.'" And the people were faint. But Jonathan said, "My father has troubled the land. Look now, how my countenance has brightened because I tasted a little of this honey. How much better if the people had eaten freely today of the spoil of their enemies which they found! For now would there not have been a much greater slaughter among the Philistines?"
>
> —I SAMUEL 14:24–30

Understand Commitment and Motivation

Why a section on harshness in a chapter about commitment and motivation? Harshness is a barrier to building true commitment. It is also a great contrast to see how King Saul put harsh and unnecessary requirements on people, whereas King David in the previous section sought to build broad-based commitment. Saul's harsh requirements reduced the people's effectiveness that day and later caused the people to cry out against the consequences of his harshness that could have led to Jonathan's death for violating an unknown requirement. (See verses 43–45.) Saul followed a pattern of coerciveness in his leadership style, and there is much evidence the people followed him less willingly than they followed David. In business, it can be easy to react to difficult situations with an autocratic "do it my way" response, but you may gain immediate action at the expense of commitment, loyalty, and even people's better judgment. Dedicate yourself to building commitment—and guard against giving directives others may view as harsh. This approach may take more time, but it is worth it in the long run.

Live It

- Beware of situations where you feel anxious, frustrated, or angry; they are ripe for you to respond harshly if you are not careful.

- Pray about difficult situations, asking for God's help and seeking His peace—this process alone will calm you down and may open your mind and spirit to other options you have not yet considered.

- Be sensitive to indications people are uncomfortable around you or seem hesitant to follow your instructions; there is a problem you need to address.

- If you make a mistake and take harsh action, be quick to apologize and dedicate yourself to follow through and restore relationships and commitment.

97

See It

Shortly after a merger between former competitors, some significant differences in style and approach began to surface and cause strife. The differences ranged from how leaders were expected to engage with customers, to how decisions should be made, to how the leadership team should operate.

The top executive, chosen from one of the former companies, began pushing for how his company had done things—and his way of addressing issues was in public. He wanted all the leaders to hear the same messages and their importance, which was good. However, his approach led to some heated debates. The top executive lost patience with one leader in particular, making several harsh statements in front of the entire leadership team— a group that was still getting to know one another. He took his anger to the next level and fired the leader shortly after that difficult meeting, even though the leader had a track record of producing strong results and was well respected in the company.

Although the executive had a responsibility to promote his vision, his harsh actions had a very negative impact, particularly on leaders from the other company. He immediately gained a reputation as being command-and-control, close-minded, harsh, and insensitive. No one dared to raise a differing point of view for fear of severe consequences. Secretly, many of the leaders began to seek new opportunities, and less than one year later, more than half of the original leadership team had left the organization and taken valuable knowledge, skills, and contacts with them. Had the executive taken actions with the goal of building commitment in his new leadership team, the outcome may have been much more positive.

CONCLUSION

As a business leader, it is vital to understand commitment and motivation in the workplace. This is a complex topic because humans are complex creatures given a free will by God. Now with an established foundation, let's move into the next chapter where we explore the techniques for building commitment and motivation.

chapter eight

BUILD COMMITMENT AND MOTIVATION
Promote willing action from others

A S DISCUSSED IN chapter 7, commitment is an essential ingredient for effective business results. People must be motivated to regularly make the right decisions and take the right actions without the need for constant supervision—otherwise, the organization's productivity and results will suffer. Actively weave commitment tactics into your everyday work, and you will have a direct and positive impact on people's commitment and motivation to the business and its results. These tactics take a little extra time and effort on the front end, but they will pay off handsomely—and enhance how you are perceived as a leader.

SEEK OPPORTUNITIES FOR OTHERS TO PARTICIPATE

At the time of this story, Jesus was well known, and a significant number of disciples followed Him. The twelve apostles were active in preaching and healing activities, and Jesus mentored them as well as other disciples.

> When the day began to wear away, the twelve came and said to Him, "Send the multitude away, that they may go into the surrounding towns and country, and lodge and get provisions; for we are in a deserted place here." But He said to them, "You give them something to eat." And they said, "We have no more than five loaves and two fish, unless we go and buy food for all these people." For there were about five thousand men. And He said to His disciples, "Make them sit down in groups of fifty." And they did so, and made them all sit down. Then He took the five loaves and the two fish, and

99

LEAD AND SUCCEED

looking up to heaven, He blessed and broke them, and gave them to the disciples to set before the multitude. So they all ate and were filled, and twelve baskets of the leftover fragments were taken up by them.

—LUKE 9:12–17

After these things the Lord appointed seventy others also, and sent them two by two before His face into every city and place where He Himself was about to go.

—LUKE 10:1

Participation is a powerful tactic that can be used for building commitment and motivation—and perhaps the tactic you should use most often. In Luke 9, Jesus could have resolved the issue by Himself—He did not need the disciples' involvement. However, Jesus chose to involve the disciples in tasks from reporting on the issue to executing His "miracle food" strategy. Jesus's approach to this opportunity went beyond simple delegation. All were involved in the activities themselves and in sharing the results that were achieved. When you involve people in important tasks, you give them the chance to feel good about their contributions—and to the results they helped to generate. Also, Jesus got people involved from the very beginning of some activities, which gave them a strong sense of ownership for the work and for doing what was necessary to make it succeed.

Live It

- Recognize that participation is a powerful building block for commitment and motivation.

- Carefully consider your best role, and guard against immediately taking action when people bring problems to you; you may miss an opportunity to involve others.

- Ask others to research the problems or opportunities and to develop recommendations.

Build Commitment and Motivation

- Give others latitude to participate in the decision process and even to decide what to do; this may be the best way to build their commitment to the decision (as long as you remember not to overturn the decision you've agreed to delegate).

- Look for ways even more people can participate in implementing the decisions—giving them the authority to design the details within certain boundaries.

- Bring things full circle: use thought-provoking questions to ask people what they learned and how they can apply it to the future.

See It

On a major effort, the senior sponsors were worried about a particular group of leaders who were negative about the transformation. They were pivotal to the success, so a consulting team was asked to explore the issue and develop a way to address it.

In meeting with representatives of the negative group, it was clear there were many unaddressed issues, and few had been fixed. The consultants knew the situation represented an opportunity disguised as a challenge. They met with the senior sponsors to communicate what they uncovered, and they proposed a solution. The sponsors took the advice and launched an advisory board. Members of the negative group were invited to participate along with others. Their role was to explore and address the many issues they faced together. Members of the board were required to meet with others between meetings to uncover and understand the issues, gain ideas for addressing them, and research various alternatives. The board was also given decision authority in a number of important areas and resources to implement their proposed solutions. Over time, membership in the advisory board became viewed as an honor, and many of the complaints were resolved with high satisfaction because of the important participation offered to key people in the organization.

LEAD AND SUCCEED

RECOGNIZE APPROPRIATE LIMITS OF PARTICIPATION

The placement of this story in the Gospels tends to indicate it happened relatively early in Jesus's three-year ministry. At the time of this story, the twelve apostles had been identified, and Jesus was widely known for His healing miracles.

And behold, one of the rulers of the synagogue came, Jairus by name. And when he saw Him, he fell at His feet and begged Him earnestly, saying, "My little daughter lies at the point of death. Come and lay Your hands on her, that she may be healed, and she will live." So Jesus went with him, and a great multitude followed Him and thronged Him....

While He was still speaking, some came from the ruler of the synagogue's house who said, "Your daughter is dead. Why trouble the Teacher any further?" As soon as Jesus heard the word that was spoken, He said to the ruler of the synagogue, "Do not be afraid; only believe." And He permitted no one to follow Him except Peter, James, and John the brother of James. Then He came to the house of the ruler of the synagogue, and saw a tumult and those who wept and wailed loudly. When He came in, He said to them, "Why make this commotion and weep? The child is not dead, but sleeping." And they ridiculed Him. But when He had put them all outside, He took the father and the mother of the child, and those who were with Him, and entered where the child was lying. Then He took the child by the hand, and said to her, "Talitha, cumi," which is translated, "Little girl, I say to you, arise." Immediately the girl arose and walked, for she was twelve years of age. And they were overcome with great amazement. But He commanded them strictly that no one should know it, and said that something should be given her to eat.

—MARK 5:22–24, 35–43

102

Build Commitment and Motivation

Participation is a great technique for building commitment, and Jesus used it extensively with His disciples. However, here is an example when Jesus limited the participation of even His closest twelve. For business leaders, the important fact is He did not include everyone in this endeavor. Also, He did not apologize for the limitations, nor did He even explain Himself in what the Bible has captured about the event. The truth is that some business tasks are simply best handled with limited participation. Examples include designing organization structures, making leadership assignments, handling sensitive legal issues, and the like. If you regularly use broad-based participation—but carefully limit involvement in complex, difficult, or "vested stake" situations— you will build commitment but not be hampered by involvement that can delay, or actually impede, progress at times.

Live It

- Recognize it is a more common mistake for leaders to limit participation when it could be beneficial than to use participation when it may become a hindrance.

- Consider what you are trying to achieve and how involving others will impact it.
    - Do people have a vested stake in the outcome such that they may want to push strongly for their preference?
    - Do they have important knowledge and skills you need to complete the work most effectively?
    - How could their participation help or hinder the outcome and timeliness of decisions or results?

- Use these insights to decide the best participation approach.

- Identify the people you want to involve and the specific roles you want them to take.

- Communicate the roles to those involved and to appropriate others—and be sure to clarify expectations that are both inside and outside their role to guard against misunderstandings.

LEAD AND SUCCEED

- Consider whether you should explain the reasons for your participation decisions (for example, to squelch rumors or concerns), but do not feel the need to make excuses for decisions you believe are right.

See It

The information services group for a manufacturing company was making some radical changes. The CIO admitted to waiting too long to make several needed changes. He had a participative style of leadership and encouraged broad participation in virtually everything—and sought consensus among his leadership team on key decisions. Unfortunately, this was a key factor in how the organization got into their predicament. On the most important and difficult areas they needed to address, they could not reach consensus, so little or nothing happened.

Among the many changes needed was a difficult organizational restructure. The group's structure had remained unchanged—and with most of the same leaders—for several years. Now many of the "comfortable" aspects of the structure would change—significantly. The CIO explained to me how he preferred to involve his entire leadership team in designing the details for the new organization structure. It was consistent with his overall leadership style, so the team would expect it.

But as we discussed some of the key criteria for the new structure, the problems we would encounter became clear. First, the future leadership team would be smaller, so not everyone would have a place at the leader "table," and some of those leaders who would lose a seat would report to others who had been their peers. Also, this was the same leadership team that had failed to agree on previous changes, including similar restructuring attempts.

To address these issues, I suggested that we identify the top three leaders—the ones who would hold the top three positions in the new organization structure—and work with them. This approach required the CIO to determine which position each top leader would hold in the new structure. I told him this was necessary to prevent them from worrying or jockeying for positions yet open to debate. It was clearly a different approach—and the CIO admitted he was not fully comfortable with it—but he agreed. The new organization structure was developed quickly—and much more easily than

104

Build Commitment and Motivation

even smaller changes had been in the past. With the structure designed, the first action was to communicate with the rest of the leaders. The CIO met one-on-one with each leader, giving each the chance to ask questions and express concerns. The new structure was then rolled out in "town hall" communication sessions that allowed the broader group to raise concerns and get their questions answered. After about three months, the initial concerns had calmed down, and the organization was functioning effectively in the new structure. The CIO told me later that he had learned the importance of modifying his style to meet different needs—and how too much of a good thing, like consensus, can get in the way of business results.

BALANCE THE MOTIVATIONAL ELEMENTS OF YOUR MESSAGES

Deuteronomy is a book of God's laws given to the Israelites through Moses while they were in the wilderness. Although framed as commandments, it reflects God's desire for relationship with Israel and provides great examples of how to communicate requirements within a "pull" commitment strategy, as discussed in chapter 7.

> Now it shall come to pass, if you diligently obey the voice of the LORD your God, to observe carefully all His commandments which I command you today, that the LORD your God will set you high above all nations of the earth. And all these blessings shall come upon you and overtake you, because you obey the voice of the LORD your God: Blessed shall you be in the city, and blessed shall you be in the country. Blessed shall be the fruit of your body, the produce of your ground and the increase of your herds, the increase of your cattle and the offspring of your flocks. Blessed shall be your basket and your kneading bowl. Blessed shall you be when you come in, and blessed shall you be when you go out....
>
> But it shall come to pass, if you do not obey the voice of the LORD your God, to observe carefully all His commandments and His statutes which I command you today, that all these curses will come upon you and overtake you:

105

LEAD AND SUCCEED

Cursed shall you be in the city, and cursed shall you be in the country. Cursed shall be your basket and your kneading bowl. Cursed shall be the fruit of your body and the produce of your land, the increase of your cattle and the offspring of your flocks. Cursed shall you be when you come in, and cursed shall you be when you go out.

—DEUTERONOMY 28:1–6, 15–19

Read the entire chapter of Deuteronomy 28 to see the full details of the blessings and curses God laid out for the Israelites.

When using communications to build motivation, the best strategy is to combine messages that answer both "What will I gain if I do this?" and "What will I lose if I don't?" In general, more people are compelled to act by "loss" messages than by "gain" messages, so the balance needs to be tipped toward those messages even though they are more difficult to deliver. In Deuteronomy 28, just fourteen verses are dedicated to the "gain" messages while fifty-four are dedicated to the "loss" messages—an approximate 80/20 split. The rule of thumb I like to use is to concentrate these messages approximately 60–80 percent in favor in "loss" messages, leaning toward 80 percent when the messages are vitally important, as demonstrated in Deuteronomy. Also, notice the message details are very specific. Vague messages at a high level—such as information about improving customer satisfaction or the company's financial condition—won't have the same motivational impact as messages that clearly answer "what is in it for me" (WIIFM). Follow God's example about "gain" and "loss" messages, enough detail, and focus on WIIFM to build motivation for the actions necessary for success.

Live It

- Identify the actions you need others to take—and avoid—and how these actions differ from what people are doing today.

- Identify the positive outcomes from these actions and the negative outcomes from failing to take them (or for contrary action).

106

Build Commitment and Motivation

- Consider the organization, the people, and what types of messages will be especially motivational.

- Develop messages that convey the benefits and positive outcomes from these actions—for the customers, company, department, and individuals, putting particular emphasis on the team and individual levels; for example:
  - More satisfied customers—going beyond what competitors can do
  - Improved financial position for the company
  - Increased potential for business unit sales and revenues
  - Fewer customer complaints to handle
  - Reduced "busy work" and greater sense of accomplishment
  - More career opportunities
  - Increased raise and bonus potential

- Develop messages that convey the problems and negative outcomes from failing to take the actions or taking contrary action—with strong emphasis on the team and individual level; for example:
  - Increased customer frustration about unmet needs
  - Decreased brand image for the company and loss of market share
  - Fewer opportunities to sell into new or existing markets
  - Continued frustrations with problem areas and customer complaints
  - Increased unpaid overtime to keep up with requirements
  - Reduced opportunity for raises and bonuses
  - Fewer career opportunities or potential for advancement

- For negative consequences, communicate the undesirable effects that are inherent in the situation rather than direct punishment unless the situation calls for it (for example, legal or ethical failure).

LEAD AND SUCCEED

- Determine the best mix of messages—recognizing that different people will gravitate to different messages as being most important and motivating.

- Resist the urge to emphasize the "gain" messages simply because they are easier to deliver; in general, they will create less motivation than "loss" messages.

- Determine the best ordering of your messages.
  - Deliver "gain" messages first when people are experiencing current problems to bring hope and set an initial positive tone to keep people engaged.
  - Deliver "loss" messages first when there is little awareness or understanding of the problem or opportunity.

See It

One company president had a daunting task. He needed to motivate his top leaders to take on a significant enterprise-wide project right after the completion of the last one. We spoke with him about his last project and learned it had been highly successful, so we delivered news he didn't expect: the high success of the last project was a problem for building motivation for his new one. People were pleased, satisfied, and content—not the best breeding ground for motivating extra efforts again so soon.

We worked with the president to identify the right "gain" and "loss" messages for the new project. Then we asked him about his top leaders. What types of situations provoked responses from them? What would cause them to feel a strong sense of urgency? There was no question in his mind: it was marketplace competition. We then showed the president how to use this natural motivator to craft his "gain" and "loss" messages to get their attention. Each of his messages had a strong tie to marketplace competition and strongly implied stock price changes—strongly motivational because the top leaders' received stock as a significant part of their compensation. The president applied his own style in crafting his messages. He chose to use rhetorical questions to lead others to their own views on how the company would lose out if they didn't take action right then, and how there was significant potential to grow more market share if they moved forward quickly.

108

Build Commitment and Motivation

The president called a special meeting of his top leaders and began by congratulating them on their recent success, mentioning how it had significantly propelled their market position. It was a great celebration with cheering and lots of smiles. Then he asked his "loss" rhetorical questions to get their attention. "As you know, we finally have a place at the table in terms of market share. And we could be very satisfied with that. But what if every competitor in our industry spends the same percentage of revenues on advertising and R&D; who will be on top—and stay on top?"

As an observer, I was able to see physical signs of discomfort in the room—the beginnings of motivation. People were literally squirming, putting hands to their faces in obvious contemplation, and looking at one another with furrowed brows. Then the president mentioned the project and the key "gain" messages associated with it. The results were immediate—a unanimous acceptance of the new project by these critical sponsors. Over a few years, the project, although extremely difficult, did exactly what the president said. Their marketplace position grew significantly, and those results were quickly achieved because the president had built motivation at a time when it was not naturally easy to build.

CELEBRATE KEY MILESTONES

In the final stages of Israel's time of slavery in Egypt, God instituted Passover as a way of commemorating His deliverance. The final plague, when Passover first began, resulted in the death angel killing the firstborn of the Egyptians. The Israelites had followed God's commands and were passed over and spared from the tragedy.

And Moses said to the people: "Remember this day in which you went out of Egypt, out of the house of bondage; for by strength of hand the LORD brought you out of this place. No leavened bread shall be eaten. On this day you are going out, in the month Abib. And it shall be, when the LORD brings you into the land of the Canaanites and the Hittites and the Amorites and the Hivites and the Jebusites, which He swore to your fathers to give you, a land flowing with milk and honey, that you shall keep this service in this month. Seven

109

LEAD AND SUCCEED

days you shall eat unleavened bread, and on the seventh day there shall be a feast to the LORD. Unleavened bread shall be eaten seven days. And no leavened bread shall be seen among you, nor shall leaven be seen among you in all your quarters. And you shall tell your son in that day, saying, 'This is done because of what the LORD did for me when I came up from Egypt.' It shall be as a sign to you on your hand and as a memorial between your eyes, that the LORD's law may be in your mouth; for with a strong hand the LORD has brought you out of Egypt. You shall therefore keep this ordinance in its season from year to year."

—EXODUS 13:3–10

God wanted the Israelites—including later generations—to know about the miracle of the first Passover. Companies have special moments as well. These moments should be recognized and celebrated because they are like family traditions: they build a special feeling and generate a sense of membership not easily generated any other way. Regularly celebrating key events and their significance makes people feel like they are a part of something desirable, and it helps to reinforce the organization's culture for new people. Recognizing an organization's history and legacy can also lead to true loyalty within the workforce.

Key milestones come in all types, such as the company's launch, date of going public, date of a merger or spin-off, and date of achieving a key organizational goal. You can use a variety of symbols and events to keep them fresh in people's minds and in the stories people tell. Use the power of celebrating milestones, and you'll promote lasting commitment to the organization.

Live It

- Acknowledge the key milestones and events that have helped to define your organization, department, or team.

- Find ways to recognize key successes, such as anniversary celebrations, banners with names of project participants, and plaques about key milestones.

Build Commitment and Motivation

- View these celebrations as a way to communicate with new employees and draw them into the culture.

- Encourage people to share their own stories about these important events; it may build traditions that can hold the organization and its people together.

See It

Communities of practice (Cops) are one way to encourage knowledge transfer in an organization. Cops are typically informal, voluntary groups of people around a topic of interest. They are often reliant on the passion and commitment of the original leaders to keep them going.

One such CoP benefited from its passionate leaders and from the fact that the leaders genuinely enjoyed being together when they met periodically. At one of the first gatherings, a ritual was born that became a rite of passage for new leaders as they joined. It all began during a dinner meeting, where two people realized they had something in common: attending camp as children and singing silly camp songs with hand gestures. They started to sing one of the songs, along with its gestures—and the rest of the leaders stopped to find out what they were doing. Soon everyone was learning the song and enjoying the moment. At their next meeting, someone requested the song.

That began multiple years commemorating the launch of the CoP, with the song at the center. New verses were also written about key milestones and events during the life of the CoP. The song—or rather the tradition of the song—celebrated the life and development of the CoP and contributed to a strong sense of membership and camaraderie among the leaders. This was important because much of the CoP's work was voluntary and relied on the passion the leaders poured into—and derived from—work outside their regular job responsibilities.

MAKE APPROPRIATE ASSURANCES

Noah and his ark saved eight people and the world's animal species from God's judgment in a worldwide flood. The Flood itself lasted for one hundred fifty days (Genesis 7:24), so Noah and his family may have been on the ark for over a year before the water receded. During this time, they had the task

LEAD AND SUCCEED

of caring for and living with the animals, awaiting an unknown future of rebuilding and repopulating the land that had been destroyed.

> Then God spoke to Noah and to his sons with him, saying: "And as for Me, behold, I establish My covenant with you and with your descendants after you, and with every living creature that is with you: the birds, the cattle, and every beast of the earth with you, of all that go out of the ark, every beast of the earth. Thus I establish My covenant with you: Never again shall all flesh be cut off by the waters of the flood; never again shall there be a flood to destroy the earth." And God said: "This is the sign of the covenant which I make between Me and you, and every living creature that is with you, for perpetual generations: I set My rainbow in the cloud, and it shall be for the sign of the covenant between Me and the earth. It shall be, when I bring a cloud over the earth, that the rainbow shall be seen in the cloud; and I will remember My covenant which is between Me and you and every living creature of all flesh; the waters shall never again become a flood to destroy all flesh."
>
> —GENESIS 9:8–15

Difficult actions—such as restructuring and layoffs—are unfortunately frequent in today's business environment. When they are necessary, leaders need to complete these difficult actions all at once—and give assurances—to the best of their ability. Notice in this case, God took a complete action by sending the Flood, and He assured Noah and his family that another flood would never happen. Obviously such solid assurances are not possible in today's business climate, but expressing your intent can be very helpful. Without God's assurances, it is unlikely Noah would have wanted to venture very far from that ark—just in case—and his overall responsibility of rebuilding and repopulating the earth could have been severely impacted. Every time it rained, those who had experienced the Flood—or had heard about it—would likely have been filled with great anxiety that could have crippled their ability to act.

112

Build Commitment and Motivation

If you are a leader at a time of difficult actions, you'll want your organization to rebound quickly into the new reality. One way to help them is to find ways to assure them—and a foundation for this is to ensure you have completed the action. This is especially important in difficult work such as layoffs. A steady "drip" of difficult actions that are perceived negatively can reduce loyalty and impact productivity as people become preoccupied with their own protection and interests. Of course, if your company is facing an ongoing need for difficult actions, you'll want to express that to people and encourage them to roll up their sleeves and help. But if your company is continuing to take difficult actions and is not facing a crisis of some nature, you may want to explore why. Is there inadequate planning? Are people taking short-term actions at the expense of the long term? Dedicate yourself to taking complete actions and to providing some degree of assurance. It will help you to overcome one source of reduced commitment and motivation.

Live It

- Recognize the potential for long-term negative impact when you must take difficult actions.

- Invite God into the situation by seeking His wisdom and will in prayer.

- Put yourself in the shoes of those impacted to get a balanced view; for instance, following a layoff announcement, it is important to be sensitive to those leaving the business as well as acknowledge the pain felt by "survivors."

- Do everything possible to take all the needed action at once; you'll avoid the syndrome of "death by a thousand cuts" and the divided focus and preoccupation that come with it.

- Identify information you can share about the future, specifically looking for any assurances you can comfortably make to allay concerns.

- Ask God to give you compassion, credibility, and favor as you deliver the messages.

LEAD AND SUCCEED

- Follow up with influencers and key people one-on-one to take a pulse on the mood and morale, and to seek their help in understanding and managing the situation.

- Deliver additional messages using a variety of communications to increase confidence among people.

See It

A services firm had a no-layoff policy, which had worked well for its relatively stable set of services. However, over the prior three years, the company had grown significantly, especially in some new service areas that were more responsive to market ups and downs. Unfortunately, the market had shifted for its new services. Being new to the services, the company found itself less able to sell in a down market, so it was significantly overstaffed. Believing he had some terrific people on board and wanting to maintain the no-layoff policy, the president extended an offer for a voluntary six-month sabbatical at 20 percent pay. Unfortunately, few people took the offer, so some people were put on involuntary six-month sabbatical. After those six months, it was clear the market had not turned around, so the company implemented its first layoff of 10 percent of the workforce. The president communicated that this should be the only layoff because they had taken steps to cut deeply.

However, this proved not to be the case. Only a few months later, the company did another significant layoff—then another. The leaders for the new service division were concerned about the president's actions and the fact he was not consulting them about the market and what they should do. Many of the sales leaders became extremely concerned and left the business. Without enough sales to keep people busy, there were two more layoffs.

The company—including its core services—was decimated and forced to close many offices. Although the president did the right thing by attempting to give assurances, he found how difficult it can be to make assurances in conditions he could not control and frankly did not understand. The company started with a difficult policy—the no-layoff policy—that did not help them in those market conditions. The president also failed to involve others in producing realistic, and even pessimistic, predictions of sales, which could have helped them to better understand and communicate expectations. Perhaps with better involvement and more realistic planning and messaging,

Build Commitment and Motivation

the entire company could have been spared the full extent of the negative impacts they ultimately faced.

CONCLUSION

The Bible has much to say about building commitment and motivation in people—all of which can be leveraged at work. Keep the need for commitment and motivation in mind, and apply these techniques to make them a reality. You will build a more productive and satisfying workplace with people who willingly achieve the targeted business results.

chapter nine

UNDERSTAND COMMUNICATION FUNDAMENTALS
Learn from biblical communication examples

O F ALL THE important activities leaders perform, communications are probably the most frequent. Some people think of communications narrowly—for instance, formal communications such as presentations, e-mails, and Web sites. However, you'll be most effective when you remember communication is much more than simply transmitting messages you want others to know. Communications require you to constantly adopt a role of both sender and receiver, and to establish a context to help others truly "get" what they need to know. The Bible is full of communication examples for leaders to explore. In fact, the Bible itself is an overall communication from God. This chapter builds a foundation for communications, and chapter 10 goes further to provide a series of communication techniques to follow.

REMEMBER THE OTHER PART OF COMMUNICATION
James was the leader of the Christian council in Jerusalem. In the Gospels, he was identified as the brother of Jesus. Although not one of the twelve apostles, James was a central figure in the early days of the Christian church.

> So then, my beloved brethren, let every man be swift to hear, slow to speak, slow to wrath.
>
> —JAMES 1:19

It can be easy for leaders to forget that a key aspect of communication is listening. Communication cannot be considered complete—let

LEAD AND SUCCEED

alone effective—if you cannot be certain the message was received. This
requires listening. Also, much of the communication leaders do is to motivate specific action. Without listening, you may miss that the receiver
has input or questions—and you may assume all is well right up to the
moment things do not go as planned. A dedication to listening starts with
an acknowledgment: leaders often need to hear *from* people as much (and
even more) than they need to tell people something. Leaders who are dedicated to listening will hear information they may not discover any other
way. This passage puts things into perspective by listing hearing first, thus
encouraging people to make it a priority over speaking. As my husband
wisely mentioned one day, "We have two ears and one mouth and need to
use them in proportion."

Live It

- Dedicate yourself to listening as a top priority in your
  communications—and be sure to give people the right opportunity to share their feedback and thoughts by devoting
  specific time to it.

- Remember communication takes place continually and not
  simply during formal, planned events and through frequently
  used tools such as e-mail.

- Keep two-way exchange in mind: know what messages you
  want to deliver, what questions you want to ask, and how you
  will make listening an active part of the exchange.

- Select venues that support two-way communications for key
  messages, such as meetings and phone calls instead of e-mail
  and Web sites.

- Consider whether you should start by listening to others first
  rather than delivering your messages; it can be especially
  valuable in difficult or contentious situations or when it is
  vital you understand the circumstances well before you let
  others know your decision or thoughts on the topic.

118

Understand Communication Fundamentals

- Identify possible responses or questions that may arise, and be ready for them—recognizing your initial response will set the tone for the rest of the discussion.

- Recognize many people are uncomfortable with stating their views, so you may want to consider the venue (for example, people may speak more readily in a small group) and even mention what the people could be thinking but may be uncomfortable to raise on their own.

See It

One project team discovered how a leader who fails to listen can be a bigger hindrance than help. This project's sponsor was the key decision maker, but he had a number of other pressing priorities and was not close to the project's details. The team was capable but needed help at times. When the team met with the sponsor to discuss problems and get his help, the sponsor would listen for only a few minutes and then quickly give directives. Repeatedly, his instructions required the team to explore the feasibility of the solutions he offered, but rarely were they effective for the problem the team brought forward. Instead, these interactions wasted time, extended the project schedule, and frustrated the team.

Eventually, the team solicited the sponsor's executive assistant. They asked him to become familiar with project details and help get the sponsor to slow down and listen to the issues and requests before making decisions. The executive assistant was very helpful because he was well respected by the executive and knowledgeable of the executive's priorities, so this "fix" worked well. However, the executive could have enhanced his results—and the team's results—by making listening a higher priority in his leadership style.

EXPLAIN "WHY"

These passages come from the Sermon on the Mount. Due to its placement in the Gospels, it is reasonable to assume this sermon occurred relatively early in Jesus's ministry.

119

LEAD AND SUCCEED

> You have heard that it was said, "You shall love your neighbor and hate your enemy." But I say to you, love your enemies, bless those who curse you, do good to those who hate you, and pray for those who spitefully use you and persecute you, that you may be sons of your Father in heaven; for He makes His sun rise on the evil and on the good, and sends rain on the just and on the unjust. For if you love those who love you, what reward have you? Do not even the tax collectors do the same? And if you greet your brethren only, what do you do more than others? Do not even the tax collectors do so? Therefore you shall be perfect, just as your Father in heaven is perfect.
>
> —MATTHEW 5:43–48

Many leaders neglect an important element of effective communication: the reason. Here, Jesus could have easily said, "Love your enemies...because I said so." But He went further and explained why—and His "why" was in a good amount of detail. Jesus knew people respond better to directions when they understand why they are important—and the implicit or explicit benefits of doing them. Take the time to consistently add the "why" explanations to your communications. You will find people better understand what you want for them to do and may even adopt new beliefs that will help them to follow through readily in the future.

Live It

- Identify the actions you want people to take, or avoid, and why they are important.

- Don't assume others agree with you; they may be pulling for a different solution, and your rationale may need to be strong enough to overcome their current point of view.

- Craft messages that explain why the actions are important— and put yourself "in the shoes" of the listeners so you can develop a message that speaks to each unique perspective.

120

Understand Communication Fundamentals

- Identify the best way to deliver your message—and recognize that personal communications, such as face-to-face meetings and phone calls, may be best to explain your rationale convincingly.

- Consider delivering your message in multiple ways to convey its importance.

- Promote two-way dialogue; it will help you recognize how people are responding and whether they understand your expectations and why they are important.

- Identify ways to test for awareness and understanding, and remember that asking thought-provoking questions is frequently a good choice.

- Recognize the "why" can get lost over time, especially during a lengthy transformation, so reinforce the rationale periodically.

See It

After acquiring two former competitors, a parent company found a significant difference in employee acceptance based on how well the leaders had explained the reasons for selling their companies. In the months leading up to the acquisitions, both of the soon-to-be acquired companies were struggling financially and had communicated openly with employees about the need to take significant action. However, one of the companies was far more open with employees about what lay ahead and the reasons they needed to take difficult actions.

Once the deals were announced, but before they were completed, both companies' leadership teams sent messages to employees about the reasons for the deals, but those messages were quite different. The company that had been more open with employees before the deal continued that pattern and focused a great amount of attention on why the sale was necessary and how it would be the best way to preserve what they had built together. The leaders for this company crafted their messages for the employees, carefully thinking about how the messages would be received by different levels and types of

121

LEAD AND SUCCEED

employees. The other company explained the rationale for the deal from the company's perspective—why the deal made financial sense—but provided little information about why it made sense also for employees. This contrast in communications resulted in a striking difference in how well employees accepted the deals and changes from the new parent company. One set of new employees was much better prepared by its leadership team—leaders who had taken the time to clarify the all-important "why."

ALIGN THE FULL MESSAGE

Relatively early in the forty-year journey in the wilderness, God established worship procedures for the Israelites. While slaves in Egypt, the Israelites had not engaged in active worship, so it was important for God to clearly communicate His intent and key principles to ensure people would worship Him properly.

> This is what everyone among those who are numbered shall give: half a shekel according to the shekel of the sanctuary (a shekel is twenty gerahs). The half-shekel shall be an offering to the LORD. Everyone included among those who are numbered, from twenty years old and above, shall give an offering to the LORD. The rich shall not give more and the poor shall not give less than half a shekel, when you give an offering to the LORD, to make atonement for yourselves. And you shall take the atonement money of the children of Israel, and shall appoint it for the service of the tabernacle of meeting, that it may be a memorial for the children of Israel before the LORD, to make atonement for yourselves.
>
> —EXODUS 30:13–16

God ensured there was congruence in His full message—something business leaders also need to do. In this case, God was speaking to the Israelites about atonement or forgiveness, not another type of giving (such as tithing or freewill offerings). It was important for God to communicate that everyone needs the same atonement—there aren't different degrees. If the rich were to give more than the poor, an unintended message could have been received:

Understand Communication Fundamentals

some people need more atonement for their sins than others, or perhaps it would be OK to sin because it was possible to "pay" more to be forgiven. Instead, God was careful to align His message and avoid misunderstanding by clearly saying what they should and should not do. As God demonstrated here, leaders need to recognize that they communicate messages in many different ways. You'll want to carefully examine your messages to ensure everything lines up—from what you want people to think about and prioritize to what you want them to do and not do. Taking the extra time to "pull the string" all the way through and make sure it is straight will help to reduce confusion and chances for people to take undesirable actions.

Live It

- Recognize you send "messages" in:
    - What you say and what you don't say
    - What you do and what you don't do
    - Your facial expressions and body language
    - Your degree of enthusiasm and tone of voice
    - How much time and attention you devote
    - How you respond to situations
    - Your priorities—stated and implied—by the people you assign, the decisions you make, and the resources you make available

- Examine what you want from a variety of perspectives:
    - What is most important for people to understand?
    - What actions would support this? What actions would detract from it?
    - What is your role in achieving the desired outcome?
    - How might people interpret, or misinterpret, your words and actions?
    - How are people likely to react and respond, initially and over time?
    - How could your message and corresponding actions help

LEAD AND SUCCEED

to communicate the intended result? How might your
messages and actions detract from your intentions?

- Develop what you want to say, and carefully plan how to
  align all the "messages" (for example, words, responses, body
  language, tone of voice).

- Be on the lookout for inconsistencies, and move quickly to
  resolve them.

See It

The leadership team for a multicompany venture met to discuss some
recent problems they were facing. Employees at lower levels were escalating
many issues to the leadership team—many more than either had experienced
historically—and the leaders felt inundated. "We need to tell them they are
empowered to make these decisions," one senior leader said.

Her statement was met by a question from one particularly vocal leader:
"So will we stop overriding their decisions, like we do now?" All eyes were
fixed on him, so he went on. "That's how we've gotten into this mess. This
work is complicated, and we're all doing the best we can, but let's admit that
just about every problem they've tried to handle has been overridden by us.
Why should they even bother trying to make a decision if someone is going
to change it anyway?" His bold statement set the leadership team back a bit.
However, after a discussion about some of the decisions they had changed
and why, the leaders agreed they had inadvertently caused the problem. So
they began to identify which decisions could be handled by what level of
leader or employee. After communicating these new levels of authority, the
leaders began to "self-police" to keep themselves to their agreements. In the
few instances when decisions were changed, they explored them carefully
first and then clearly communicated the reasons to those involved. It took
time to reap the benefits of their new plan, but eventually employees were
more willing to make decisions and better understood what they needed to
do. The work environment became more productive, and everyone benefited
from higher morale.

124

Understand Communication Fundamentals

REINFORCE YOUR MESSAGE VISUALLY

This passage contains instructions from God to the Israelites while in the wilderness. These instructions appear in the Bible shortly after the people believed the negative report of the ten spies instead of the faith-filled report of Joshua and Caleb about the Promised Land. It is also recorded directly after an incident where a man violated one of the commandments and was put to death.

> Speak to the children of Israel: Tell them to make tassels on the corners of their garments throughout their generations, and to put a blue thread in the tassels of the corners. And you shall have the tassel, that you may look upon it and remember all the commandments of the LORD and do them, and that you may not follow the harlotry to which your own heart and your own eyes are inclined, and that you may remember and do all My commandments, and be holy for your God.
>
> —NUMBERS 15:38–40

Symbols and other visual clues are helpful reinforcements for your messages. In this case, it was clear from two recent episodes that God needed to reinforce His commandments and their importance. First, the people had failed to follow, in faith, His instructions about taking the Promised Land. Second, a man had violated a commandment. It appeared the people might not be taking God's commandments seriously. It may have been for these reasons He chose to reinforce His expectations visually at that time. You will find that messages delivered and reinforced in multiple ways are more likely to be remembered. Some business examples include posters, laminated cards, and project logos—and even creative ideas, such as one company's distribution of sunglasses to tell employees its project would lead to an even brighter future. Use the power of visual examples to reinforce your key messages and make them really stick with people.

LEAD AND SUCCEED

Live It

- Identify creative ideas to reinforce visually, such as circumstances where people are not following through on your expectations.

- Work with others to brainstorm creative ideas for reinforcing these important messages, perhaps even delegating this task to others.

- Consider how each idea may be perceived; explore any relevant history and other insights about how people may respond to them.

- After implementing your visual, talk to people to test whether it is having the intended impact.
    - Is it reinforcing your message?
    - Is it being readily and positively received?
    - How can you apply this learning to future situations?

See It

The communications team at the Silicon Valley company wanted to convey its messages creatively. Their technology project was going to be difficult, but it would help the company reduce many repetitive tasks and free people for more value-added activities. The communications leader proposed putting messages about the project into fortune cookies. The team liked the idea, believing it would get people's attention. As one person pointed out, it is customary to show fortune cookie messages to others, so it could be a way to get people talking about the project. They moved forward with the idea and placed bowls of the cookies in various locations throughout the building. As expected, people enjoyed the messages (and the cookies!) and shared them. It was an enjoyable way to communicate messages about the project, and it built positive perceptions about the changes.

126

Understand Communication Fundamentals

LET YOUR ACTIONS REINFORCE YOUR MESSAGE

This well-known passage of Scripture communicates one of the many memorable events during the Last Supper. The Last Supper took place the night Jesus was betrayed by Judas, leading to His eventual crucifixion and resurrection.

> Jesus, knowing that the Father had given all things into His hands, and that He had come from God and was going to God, rose from supper and laid aside His garments, took a towel and girded Himself. After that, He poured water into a basin and began to wash the disciples' feet, and to wipe them with the towel with which He was girded. Then He came to Simon Peter. And Peter said to Him, "Lord, are You washing my feet?" Jesus answered and said to him, "What I am doing you do not understand now, but you will know after this." Peter said to Him, "You shall never wash my feet!" Jesus answered him, "If I do not wash you, you have no part with Me." Simon Peter said to Him, "Lord, not my feet only, but also my hands and my head!" Jesus said to him, "He who is bathed needs only to wash his feet, but is completely clean; and you are clean, but not all of you." For He knew who would betray Him; therefore He said, "You are not all clean."
>
> So when He had washed their feet, taken His garments, and sat down again, He said to them, "Do you know what I have done to you? You call me Teacher and Lord, and you say well, for so I am. If I then, your Lord and Teacher, have washed your feet, you also ought to wash one another's feet. For I have given you an example, that you should do as I have done to you."
>
> —JOHN 13:3–15

Words are important, but your messages will lack credibility if they are not accompanied by your actions. People listen to what leaders say but will judge the importance of messages based on what they see those leaders

LEAD AND SUCCEED

do. What if Jesus had simply said He wanted the disciples to serve one another? Would it have been as strong of a message? Perhaps, but it is clear from Scripture that Jesus's approach had an especially powerful impact on Peter. To be the best leader you can be, you should expect the most from yourself—to hold yourself to the highest standard. Everything you do and say—as well as *how* you do and say it—has an impact on others and conveys important messages. You can leverage this fact to great advantage by letting your actions be a strong element of your overall message.

Live It

- Objectively examine your own life.
    - How important is it for you to be a solid, consistent example for others to follow?
    - If you never said a word about important topics, what might people assume from watching what you do?
    - How consistently do you demonstrate what you expect from others?
    - Are there areas where you need to come up higher?

- Be aware that others may interpret inconsistencies between your words and actions as problems of integrity and trustworthiness, so you should take them seriously and address them.

- Make a firm, quality decision to demonstrate your expectations and begin by changing your actions—recognizing it may actually raise suspicions and draw attention to additional inconsistencies if you tell others about the change rather than simply begin to demonstrate it.

- Ask a friend or confidant to help you be aware and accountable for driving consistency between your words and actions.

See It

One of the leaders on my team called me after our regular Friday staff conference call. "I've got to tell you it's obvious you're not concentrating on

Understand Communication Fundamentals

these calls," he started. "I'm not sure what else you're doing, but if you expect us to be on the calls, you really need to be there too."

Ouch! He was right. I had made it a policy these calls were to be attended regularly, except for important priorities such as client conflicts and vacation. Our team was spread across the United States, and the meetings were a way to stay in touch with one another and keep up on important business information and decisions. I led the calls but had developed a bad habit of multitasking. (May I admit it?) I would scan e-mails, answer instant messages, and sometimes even answer phone calls, all in an attempt to use my Fridays to get everything done for the week. The leader's comments were difficult to hear, but I needed to hear them and make a number of changes to prioritize the calls just as I was asking others to do. One change was to hold the calls less frequently. If I felt pressure on Fridays, I was probably not the only one. And I made other adjustments to help me to focus on the calls, such as closing my e-mail system. I'm grateful to this outspoken leader for his candid feedback—at this time as well as others when he shared his thoughts about issues we needed to address.

CONCLUSION

Effective business leaders are also effective communicators. In fact, a deficit in communications has held back many otherwise capable leaders from advancing in their careers. The Bible provides the foundation we need to understand effective communications. With this foundation in place, let's now look at many Bible-based examples of communication techniques in the next chapter.

chapter ten

PREPARE EFFECTIVE COMMUNICATIONS
Develop and deliver messages that "hit the mark"

B UILDING ON THE fundamentals from chapter 9, you're now ready to craft your messages. Once again, the Bible provides a rich source of examples to draw into the workplace. Jesus—the Master Communicator—used a wide variety of techniques to make His messages come alive, so we'll focus much attention on Him in this chapter. You are likely to be familiar with many of the scriptures referenced, which reinforces the fact that these communications were especially memorable. Throughout this chapter, the word *listener* is used for all types of communications, even written ones. Using this mind-set is another way to help your communications "hit the mark."

USE STORIES TO CONVEY COMPLICATED TOPICS
Jesus spoke frequently to crowds of all sizes. He also spent much time teaching His twelve disciples. Jesus's example provides ideas on how stories and their explanations can be used to communicate important and complex topics.

> Then He spoke many things to them in parables, saying: "Behold, a sower went out to sow. And as he sowed, some seed fell by the wayside; and the birds came and devoured them. Some fell on stony places, where they did not have much earth; and they immediately sprang up because they had no depth of earth. But when the sun was up they were scorched, and because they had no root they withered away. And some fell among thorns, and the thorns sprang up and

LEAD AND SUCCEED

choked them. But others fell on good ground and yielded a crop: some a hundredfold, some sixty, some thirty. He who has ears to hear, let him hear!"...

"Therefore hear the parable of the sower: When anyone hears the word of the kingdom, and does not understand it, then the wicked one comes and snatches away what was sown in his heart. This is he who received seed by the wayside. But he who received the seed on stony places, this is he who hears the word and immediately receives it with joy; yet he has no root in himself, but endures only for a while. For when tribulation or persecution arises because of the word, immediately he stumbles. Now he who received seed among the thorns is he who hears the word, and the cares of this world and the deceitfulness of riches choke the word, and he becomes unfruitful. But he who received seed on the good ground is he who hears the word and understands it, who indeed bears fruit and produces: some a hundredfold, some sixty, some thirty."

—MATTHEW 13:3–9, 18–23

Read Matthew 18:21–35 and Matthew 25:1–13 to see more examples of Jesus's use of stories.

Jesus told vivid stories rich with visual images for people to remember. He also went further and explained His stories at times to ensure His messages were understood. People remember stories because of the visual images they create in their minds. In fact, storytelling in business is a well-recognized way that information—as well as business culture—is transmitted. Make a decision to use stories often. You will find your messages will be interesting as well as effective, and you are likely to earn a reputation as a great communicator.

Live It

- Consider the message you want to communicate.
  - Does your message require people to think differently about a topic?

132

Prepare Effective Communications

- Is the topic complex?
- Is the topic familiar to the listeners? What do they already understand, and what might they currently misunderstand?
- If you simply tell people about the topic, do you run the risk that listeners will fail to fully understand your message or be unable to act on it?

- Brainstorm some possible stories.
  - Have you experienced something similar in the past?
  - Have you read or heard another's story you can talk about?
  - Does the situation lend itself to making up a story?

- Craft your story, using vivid language, rhetorical questions, and enough detail to convey the message, yet be brief so people can easily remember it.

- Test your message with a friendly audience.
  - Did they understand your story and its connection to your key message?
  - Did they need additional explanation?
  - Do they have suggestions to refine your story, the details, or your delivery?

See It

In 2002 and 2003, I led a development effort resulting in a service innovation—a set of new capabilities to address business culture challenges. The most novel concept and technique is a way to understand and address culture clash—a capability we titled "Right vs. Right."[1] The concept is easy to understand at a high level: it is simply conflicting right answers. But I needed a way to help audiences quickly understand the importance of the topic for their businesses—a challenge proving to be more difficult. As I considered alternate ways to communicate Right vs. Right, an overseas business trip gave me the story. Now, rather than describing Right vs.

LEAD AND SUCCEED

Right in detail, I use various versions of the following vignette, depending on my audience.

"What side of the road do they drive on in the United Kingdom (or Japan, or Australia)? So imagine one hundred people from the UK and one hundred people from the USA transported in their cars to an unknown city. Then, without any instructions, we tell them to drive. What will happen? Wrecks? Hurt people? Frustration? Well, this is Right vs. Right." Through this story, I'm able to convey the issue, often with humor from the audience. I can also engage the audience directly in answering the questions and even extend it into an interactive story if I'm trying to help the audience see the fuller ramifications. After telling it, I've heard many people refer to the "car story," which means it is communicating the message in a memorable way.

CONSIDER ANALOGIES TO CONVEY CHARACTERISTICS

Jesus spoke repeatedly about the kingdom of heaven—it was one of His most important messages. To help communicate characteristics about the kingdom, Jesus frequently used analogies such as these two.

> Another parable He put forth to them, saying: "The kingdom of heaven is like a mustard seed, which a man took and sowed in his field, which indeed is the least of all the seeds; but when it is grown it is greater than the herbs and becomes a tree, so that the birds of the air come and nest in its branches."
>
> Another parable He spoke to them: "The kingdom of heaven is like leaven, which a woman took and hid in three measures of meal till it was all leavened."
>
> —Matthew 13:31–33

Jesus used common items as examples for principles He wanted to convey. Notice He was careful to establish the context for these analogies—specifically the kingdom of heaven. When you follow Jesus's example and use analogies, it is vital you also ensure that the listeners are clear on the topic. Then they can know when and how to apply the analogy to their own experience and not be left wondering or run the risk of applying it inappropriately. Also notice Jesus

134

Prepare Effective Communications

used multiple analogies to explain different aspects of His complex subject. It is difficult to use too many analogies, so use them liberally.

Live It

- Consider the key elements of your topic.
  - What do listeners know about the topic?
  - What are the most notable aspects of the topic—the ones you want people to remember and act on?
- Stir your creative juices to identify some potential analogies.
  - Look through pictures; in fact, collect pictures for times like this.
  - Talk to people about the topic, and listen to what you emphasize; then ask them what they heard as most important.
  - Read articles, books, and business journals about your topic, seeking analogies to borrow.
- Test your chosen analogy with others to ensure it makes your point and to gain ideas for refining it (remember fewer words are often more memorable).
- Use pictures of the analogy in your communications; they will help the listener retain even more of your message.

See It

I recently needed to give some talks about service innovation—a relatively new area of interest. For this reason, I wanted to be extra creative, so I researched facts and figures and gathered stories to tell. But I needed an "opener"—something to gain the audiences' attention right away and help them to listen with a mind toward the opportunity and challenge of service innovation.

Over the years, I've collected pictures for just such occasions, so I sat down with my electronic file and muttered my key message under my breath: "Opportunity, but challenging...Opportunity, but challenging..." Then I found it—a picture of a beautiful pearl in an oyster. It was better than I hoped

135

because it also enabled me to emphasize another element of my message: things do not always go as planned and may evolve in an unexpected, yet valuable, direction. With the oyster and pearl featured prominently on the front page of my presentation and a special piece of jewelry around my neck, I opened my talk.

"Service innovation is like a pearl. Why? Well, how do pearls start? With an irritant that—under the right conditions—will be made into a beautiful pearl. In services, that irritant is a customer need that cannot be fulfilled with the current capabilities. And like the pearl, with time and work, a beautiful outcome can result—one that can be valuable for years to come. But the oyster doesn't produce a pearl every time. At times," showing my necklace, "a blister pearl results, which is an under-formed pearl. Although less valuable, it is beautiful and can be useful in unexpected ways."

DEMONSTRATE YOUR MESSAGE

Jesus's ministry on Earth was multifaceted. Certainly one of His key focus areas was to prepare the twelve apostles to carry the message of the gospel after His resurrection and ascension into heaven. Here is one such example of how He worked to prepare them.

> Then He came to Capernaum. And when He was in the house He asked them, "What was it you disputed among yourselves on the road?" But they kept silent, for on the road they had disputed among themselves who would be the greatest. And He sat down, called the twelve, and said to them, "If anyone desires to be first, he shall be last of all and servant of all." Then He took a little child and set him in the midst of them. And when He had taken him in His arms, He said to them, "Whoever receives one of these little children in My name receives Me; and whoever receives Me, receives not Me but Him who sent Me."
>
> —MARK 9:33–37

Jesus used many opportunities to demonstrate God's will and His expectations for the disciples. To ensure He made a lasting impression with this

Prepare Effective Communications

message, Jesus demonstrated His words. Demonstrations are especially powerful because the listener receives the message through multiple senses. Also, demonstrations can help to overcome a common tendency for listeners to instantly agree and assume they are fulfilling the expectations already (because they agree). Not only did Jesus make the point about being last and a servant of all, but He also demonstrated the depth of that expectation by showing how seemingly insignificant activities, such as welcoming and receiving a child, are considered to be extremely important for the "top" people in God's kingdom. It seems likely these expectations were not in the minds of the disciples as they argued over who was greatest. Look for opportunities to augment your words with a demonstration, and your communications will be more interesting and effective.

Live It

- Consider using a demonstration when listeners may be prone to rationalize or overlook parts of your expectations because it can get their attention.

- Identify a demonstration to augment your message.
    - What parts of your message are most important?
    - Is there a specific behavior, attitude, or mind-set you want to emphasize—or even redirect—in the listeners?
    - What example would show the extent of your expectations?

- Develop the rest of your message—and consider questions as a way to engage listeners directly with the message.

- Test your demonstration with others to ensure your key messages are apparent.

See It

Many businesspeople have read, seen, and heard about the "jar and rock" story attributed to several nameless people (for example, a philosophy professor, a time management expert, and so forth). I've heard it so many times I don't remember when I first heard it, but I do recall its impact and its message.

The demonstration involves filling the jar with a number of large rocks. Small rocks are then added to fill in around the large rock, then sand, and eventually water. Along the way the listeners are asked, "Is the jar full?" Although often agreeing it is full in the beginning, they understand the point as they see more and more going into the jar. The ultimate question: What is the meaning of the demonstration? This, of course, is where the value of the demonstration peaks. Some offer that it means there is always time to squeeze more in. However, the real point is you have to ensure the most important things—the big rocks—are put in the jar first, or else things of lesser importance will squeeze them out. It is a powerful business (and life) demonstration that makes an eloquent point.

GET ATTENTION THROUGH PROVOCATIVE STATEMENTS

Many people are familiar with the term "born-again Christian." This passage of Scripture documents the source and meaning of the phrase.

> There was a man of the Pharisees named Nicodemus, a ruler of the Jews. This man came to Jesus by night and said to Him, "Rabbi, we know that You are a teacher come from God; for no one can do these signs that You do unless God is with him." Jesus answered and said to him, "Most assuredly, I say to you, unless one is born again, he cannot see the kingdom of God." Nicodemus said to Him, "How can a man be born when he is old? Can he enter a second time into his mother's womb and be born?" Jesus answered, "Most assuredly, I say to you, unless one is born of water and the Spirit, he cannot enter the kingdom of God. That which is born of the flesh is flesh, and that which is born of the Spirit is spirit."
>
> —JOHN 3:1–6

Jesus got attention in this situation by making a seemingly impossible statement. This prompted Nicodemus to ask questions to clarify what Jesus

Prepare Effective Communications

meant. If Jesus had simply agreed with the initial statement of Nicodemus—although rightly affirming what he said—the important and rich meaning embedded in this exchange would have been lost. Nicodemus would have been left knowing no more about Jesus and His expectations than when he first spoke with Him. At times, you will need to get people's attention, and a provocative statement is one great way to do it.

Live It

- Recognize listeners can have an accurate, yet incomplete, view of your expectations; it will get their attention so they will listen to your message more closely.

- Identify a provocative statement to gain attention for your full message.
  - What part of your message are listeners likely to be missing?
  - What statement could prompt listeners to immediately ask a question—either audibly or mentally?
  - How can you clarify your provocative statement to further communicate your meaning?

- Test and refine your statement, recognizing your goal is to cause the listeners to ask questions and open their minds for the rest of what you have to say.

See It

In the early 1990s, IBM went through a "near-death" experience that prompted a massive transformation led by an outsider CEO, Lou Gerstner. Shortly into his leadership role, Gerstner made a statement to the press that was both provocative and legendary, although perhaps more so than he had intended.

"There's been a lot of speculation as to when I'm going to deliver a vision of IBM, and what I'd like to say to all of you is that the last thing IBM needs right now is a vision." His statement seemed shocking to many in the face of massive and ongoing losses the giant was facing at the time. Although the

139

reporters neglected the "right now" part of his statement and it impacted the message Gerstner was trying to send, it was still provocative and got lots of attention. It caused many outsiders to criticize his plans and even prompted IBMers to ask what Gerstner *did* have in mind for turning things around. IBM's turnaround story is now well documented—and it seems Gerstner was right. At that time, the company didn't need a *new* vision. Shortly after, the company did develop one to lead the move into e-business.[2]

REINFORCE KEY POINTS BY CONTRASTING STATEMENTS

In the last days before His crucifixion, Jesus spent time teaching the disciples in depth. In this case, Jesus was emphasizing the importance of putting His messages into practice.

> Jesus answered and said to him, "If anyone loves Me, he will keep My word; and My Father will love him, and We will come to him and make Our home with him. He who does not love Me does not keep My words; and the word which you hear is not Mine but the Father's who sent Me.
> —JOHN 14:23–24

Here Jesus reinforces His point by making His statement and then repeating the same message worded as an opposite or contrast. This contrasting statement technique is especially helpful to reinforce the main point of your messages. It does so by both the repetition and by the contrast, which helps people to envision both sides of the situation or expectation. This is an easy and valuable communication technique to ensure your listeners receive a rich understanding of your message.

Live It

- Use contrasting statements in a variety of situations, such as to:
  - Communicate a change you want people to make.
  - Emphasize especially important, or less obvious, aspects of your message.

Prepare Effective Communications

- Help listeners overcome a natural tendency to rationalize what they are doing today as consistent with your expectations (remember they are doing something that makes sense to them now).

- Consider the type of contrasting statement to use:
  - "Do–don't do" is good for pointing to specific actions.
  - "Is–isn't" is effective for framing understanding.
  - "From–to" is a great way to indicate specific changes.

- Determine the best ordering of your contrasting statements, for example:
  - "From–to" can be best for introducing a new change because it starts with today's situation.
  - "To–from" can be especially effective to emphasize parts of your message where listeners may not be fully understanding or performing your expectations.

See It

An insurance and financial services company was undergoing a change in business philosophy. Their vision was to become more client-centric and focused on relationships. To achieve their vision, they launched an initiative: "Client Relationship Management" (CRM). CRM required a number of changes, and the executives and project team wanted to make sure people would understand that some historic priorities would be changing in favor of more valuable ones in the future.

For part of their communications, they used the "from–to" technique. Among other details, the team mentioned two shifts that would take place: (1) *from* a product-centric *to* a client-focused business model, and (2) *from* a service orientation *to* a relationship orientation. In addition to these high-level expectations, they explained the future state in a number of ways to help people understand the "why" and the "how." This technique gained attention and helped to crystallize the nature and degree of the change the company was about to make.[3]

141

LEAD AND SUCCEED

USE QUESTIONS TO MAKE COMMUNICATIONS MORE CONVERSATIONAL

The apostle Paul is the writer of the Book of Romans. Here Paul uses one technique that can be used in both verbal and written communications, and it can be especially valuable for engaging listeners actively in receiving your full message.

What advantage then has the Jew, or what is the profit of circumcision? Much in every way! Chiefly because to them were committed the oracles of God. For what if some did not believe? Will their unbelief make the faithfulness of God without effect? Certainly not! Indeed, let God be true but every man a liar. As it is written: "That You may be justified in Your words, and may overcome when You are judged."

But if our unrighteousness demonstrates the righteousness of God, what shall we say? Is God unjust who inflicts wrath? (I speak as a man.) Certainly not! For then how will God judge the world? For if the truth of God has increased through my lie to His glory, why am I also still judged as a sinner? And why not say, "Let us do evil that good may come"?—as we are slanderously reported and as some affirm that we say. Their condemnation is just.

What then? Are we better than they? Not at all. For we have previously charged both Jews and Greeks that they are all under sin.

—ROMANS 3:1–9

In certain types of communications—especially written communications—it can be difficult to gauge the listeners' understanding. Here Paul needed to communicate a foundational truth—a key for understanding the rest of his message. In business, this could be analogous to communicating a business vision, mission, values, or any other core expectation. Interspersed in Paul's text are questions for that topic, along with the right answer. Business communications often end with frequently asked questions (FAQs) along with the appropriate answers. However, Paul demonstrated it may be wise to put some

142

Prepare Effective Communications

of these questions and answers into the core message, especially if they are important to full understanding. In general, questions are a beneficial communication technique, and you will increase listener understanding by using them frequently.

Live It

- Plan ahead to craft the questions and your approach to asking them.
- Determine the key aspects to highlight.
    - What are some questions the listeners may have?
    - What areas may listeners misunderstand, causing them to miss vital meaning?
    - In what areas may you need to get the listeners' attention so they will hear your full message?
- Use open-ended questions—ones that cannot be answered with a yes or no—because they cause the listeners to think more deeply.
    - If communicating verbally, plan for solid pauses after your questions (even if rhetorical) to allow the listeners time to digest the question and formulate an answer— and recognize their need to hear what you have to say next.
    - String several questions together to convey complexity or multiple sides of your topic.
    - Enable the listeners to answer your questions when appropriate, because it will help you to gauge their level of understanding and give them an opportunity to participate.

See It

Many of my business communications involve relatively new concepts. In preparing for these communications, I always comb through my message, looking for opportunities to ask questions. I've found this to be a great way

LEAD AND SUCCEED

to engage people and test if they are "with me." One of my favorite questions is, "So what?" It is a great question to move from the high level into some of the details and benefits. It is also a great way to test my own communications: if I can't answer that question myself, then I need to go back and work on my message!

One such presentation proved especially interesting as I worked to relay some new concepts to colleagues. I was communicating to people who would use the techniques with clients, so I needed them to think like consultants and understand why we handle activities in certain ways.

When I got to a key slide that communicated a surprising order to the activities, I asked, "Why should you define the future state culture before assessing the current state culture? What practical reason am I focused on when I ask this question?" At least six answers popped out quickly. I acknowledged all as good, but they were not the one I was seeking. "There is a very practical reason for you to consider as consultants. What project dynamic am I considering?" Again, more good answers, but not yet the one I wanted to be sure they understood. By then, everyone was actively engaged, and some were even excitedly saying, "Just tell us!" Once I began to hear answers that told me they were thinking like consultants, I told them the answer. "It helps to set your project scope. But so what?" Again, more comments—now more targeted at the point I wanted them to get. "With culture, you can go on and on with the analysis and examining the current state. Starting with the future state first, you can establish a scope that ensures greatest value for the client." That moment set the tone for the rest of our time together, and we all benefited from deep and lively discussions.

CONCLUSION

Spending time on your messages—crafting them for impact—is time well spent. The Bible provides examples of various communication techniques to use in making communications interesting and memorable as well as effective. Return to this chapter often, and use it to apply the Bible's wisdom to the important activity of communications.

chapter eleven

COACH, MENTOR, AND MODEL
Guide others to lasting improvements

A S MENTIONED BEFORE, it can be easy to perceive leadership as an earned privilege. You can undoubtedly point to many sacrifices to achieve your status as a leader. However, your extra efforts have led you to a responsibility to give into the lives of others. As a leader, you are always "on stage"—constantly guiding others directly or indirectly whether for the good or for the not-so-good. Follow the Bible's guidance in this chapter, and impact others in ways you'll be proud to admit.

REMEMBER YOUR ATTENTION IS A POWERFUL MOTIVATOR

Proverbs—the book of wisdom—was written by a number of authors and compiled over many years. This verse is attributed to Solomon in a section added by the men of Hezekiah, a good king who reigned in Judah more than two hundred years after Solomon.

> If a ruler pays attention to lies, all his servants become wicked.
>
> —PROVERBS 29:12

This passage reinforces an important principle of leadership: how leaders respond directly impacts future actions of followers. In this case, Solomon was referring to the impact of top leaders on lower leaders. However, this principle is true at all levels and applies to positive influences as well as negative ones. As a leader, you should carefully select your responses and be cognizant of the messages others are likely to interpret about what is

LEAD AND SUCCEED

acceptable, unacceptable, preferred, rewarded, and punished. Choose to see your every word and action as a message—and an implicit motivator for the future—and you will better communicate your expectations and help others to readily recognize what they should do.

Live It

- Remember every action you take is a "message" about your priorities and what you'll do in response to the actions of others.

- Recognize some people in business believe:
    - The ends justify the means—and a good outcome is desirable no matter what may have been compromised to get there.
    - "Good" is defined as good for them personally and not necessarily what is good for the company or others, such as customers.

- Dedicate yourself to living and working a higher way and leading others to do so as well.

- Be especially vigilant at times of transition (for example, when you are new in a leadership role) because some may use it to seek advantage—and you may find it personally difficult to take tough action.

- Be cautious of "self-promoters"—people who are especially good at telling stories showing themselves in a positive light— knowing that you are not likely to hear a balanced view.

See It

The CEO of a printing company found himself being unexpectedly coached by his consultants. As he told them, his vision was to transform the company's value proposition from "customer intimacy" to "operational excellence." He hired the consultants to guide him and asked them to help him do whatever was necessary. In the past, the company had worked carefully with its customers to understand their detailed requirements and then

146

Coach, Mentor, and Model

fulfilled those designs explicitly, which meant a custom job every time. But cost was becoming a problem, and standardization was a way to address it. They created a menu of choices from which customers could select colors, paper styles and sizes, and other details—a good variety of options, but with limits that would allow the company to standardize its processes and materials.

However, the company was still "plumbed" for the "whatever you want" model with its customers—and so was the CEO's mind-set. When the CEO awarded an employee for "going above and beyond" to meet a customer request, he unintentionally reinforced the old value proposition. The employee had gone outside the menu rather than helping the customer fulfill his requirements through the menu. After the meeting where the award was given, the consultants approached the CEO and verified he still wanted them to help him do whatever was necessary. Then they pointed out the disconnect between the vision and his recognition. At first, the CEO was admittedly annoyed, but he quickly realized the changes he needed to make. He then became an effective role model for the transformation and a spokesman for the new way of thinking. From then on, awards and formal recognition were specifically tied to how employees made a difference for customers *through* their new operational excellence approach, and eventually the new vision took hold across the company.

DON'T ASSUME THE ANSWER

Acts 10:38 sums up Jesus's ministry, pointing out He went about doing good and healing all who were oppressed by the devil through God's anointing. This story is one of several Bible accounts of Jesus healing the blind.

> Now they came to Jericho. As He went out of Jericho with His disciples and a great multitude, blind Bartimaeus, the son of Timaeus, sat by the road begging. And when he heard that it was Jesus of Nazareth, he began to cry out and say, "Jesus, Son of David, have mercy on me!" Then many warned him to be quiet; but he cried out all the more, "Son of David, have mercy on me!" So Jesus stood still and commanded him to be called. Then they called the blind man, saying

LEAD AND SUCCEED

to him, "Be of good cheer. Rise, He is calling you." And throwing aside his garment, he rose and came to Jesus. So Jesus answered and said to him, "What do you want Me to do for you?" The blind man said to Him, "Rabboni, that I may receive my sight." Then Jesus said to him, "Go your way; your faith has made you well." And immediately he received his sight and followed Jesus on the road.

—MARK 10:46–52

One necessary trait of leadership is confidence. But this confidence can sometimes cause leaders to assume that they have the best answer when a better one could exists. Blind Bartimaeus had an obvious need Jesus could address. But rather than assume what he wanted done, Jesus asked him. When it comes to issues with people, especially issues that can be taken personally, it is important to explore what they want done rather than to assume and act. You will avoid giving unwanted "help" and find yourself working together to achieve the answer—a foundation for increased trust and loyalty for the future.

Live It

- Remember confidence and experience have a "too much" side that can compel you to take unwanted or inappropriate action if you are not careful.

- Recognize others often hold differing points of view from yours, and those views may be based on important information you don't know or haven't considered yet.

- Make a habit of asking questions before making decisions— even seemingly obvious ones.

- Be open to handling things in a way that differs from your first instinct if others closer to the situation believe it is best.

- Use the opportunity and the ultimate results for your own growth—and to coach others.

See It

I'd made a mistake. By considering capabilities only, I had assigned a well-experienced consultant to a client where the working style wasn't a good match. The client had an assertive—even aggressive—style. People were expected to push their points of view and even talk over each other to get their points across. The consultant was more genteel and waited her "turn"—but her turn never seemed to come. And when she did get some words in edgewise, she was not taken seriously because she didn't make her points forcefully. Eventually the client complained.

I made an immediate trip to meet with the client to address the concerns. Several key client leaders told me they weren't getting good value from the consultant's contributions. They needed someone who was "engaged." Then I met with the consultant. Frankly, I have to admit my mind was made up before I met with her: I needed to pull her off the project and backfill with another consultant. But knowing there are at least two sides to every story, I wanted to give her the chance to tell me what happened because I knew she was concerned about how her performance was perceived.

In hearing her explanation, the style disconnect was confirmed, so I was surprised by her answer to my question of what we should do. "Let me fix this. I can fix it. Don't take me off this project before I've shown you I can fix it." She was emphatic—and assertive. She then explained to me how she planned to do it—and the coaching and help she needed from me to make it work. Then we agreed on a time frame (a short one!). I communicated our plan to the client to ensure they were OK with trying it, and they agreed. I stayed in close contact with both the client and the consultant—and things did turn around. A few weeks later, the consultant told me about an upcoming project milestone. A backfill would now be appropriate and less disruptive for the client, so we worked together on planning and handling the handover. My "obvious" answer would have been less effective overall for the client and would not have allowed the consultant to resolve the issue. Instead, we ended with a good result on all sides, and I felt relieved I hadn't simply pushed forward with my original plan.

LEAD AND SUCCEED

LEAD PEOPLE TO THEIR OWN ANSWERS

Being a "good Samaritan" is a common phrase for someone who treats another with extraordinary kindness. Here is the story of the good Samaritan. To understand the deeper meaning, it is important to note that the Samaritans were a mixed race and considered inferior by the Jews of Jesus's day. The story comes in response to a question Jesus was asked about the commandment to "Love your neighbor as yourself." The question: "Who is my neighbor?"

> Then Jesus answered and said: "A certain man went down from Jerusalem to Jericho, and fell among thieves, who stripped him of his clothing, wounded him, and departed, leaving him half dead. Now by chance a certain priest came down that road. And when he saw him, he passed by on the other side. Likewise a Levite, when he arrived at the place, came and looked, and passed by on the other side. But a certain Samaritan, as he journeyed, came where he was. And when he saw him, he had compassion. So he went to him and bandaged his wounds, pouring on oil and wine; and he set him on his own animal, brought him to an inn, and took care of him. On the next day, when he departed, he took out two denarii, gave them to the innkeeper, and said to him, 'Take care of him; and whatever more you spend, when I come again, I will repay you.' So which of these three do you think was neighbor to him who fell among the thieves?" And he said, "He who showed mercy on him." Then Jesus said to him, "Go and do likewise."
>
> —LUKE 10:30–37

In this story, Jesus interacted with a man looking for a specific answer—perhaps an answer to justify him in actions bothering his conscience. Jesus could have simply answered the question, but instead He chose to lead the man to his own conclusion. In doing so, Jesus used a story with both the best and the worst actions to take under the circumstances to show the contrast. Then He asked him to answer for himself. This technique can

150

Coach, Mentor, and Model

be especially helpful at times when people may rationalize what they are doing as "good enough." It is more difficult to continue doing something after admitting those actions are wrong. When you are asked by someone for specific direction, consider the reason behind the question. It may be best to lead the person to his or her own conclusions, and thus open the door to a self-initiated change.

Live It

- Realize there are often unspoken agendas you need to consider.

- Understand that people who come to their own conclusions are more likely to take action in line with those conclusions.

- Use questions as a way to engage others and to test understanding to know what particular areas need attention.

- Use stories, analogies, and other communication techniques as a way to emphasize information and explain your expectations.

See It

Many years ago, I was asked to lead an important task to deal with a complex requirement. Complicated and time-consuming system changes were underway, and we needed to handle things manually in the meantime. We hired a small team—with none having experience with the necessary accounting and financial requirements.

To teach the team, I could have demonstrated the work and taken on the most complex cases myself. However, I felt it would be best if everyone understood the underlying financial agreements, transactions, and other information. So I established a regular team meeting to review complex situations and learn together. My goal was to let the team come to their own conclusions, which meant I needed to resist the temptation to jump in too quickly to explain things.

Not only was the approach extremely effective in quickly teaching the needed knowledge and skills, but it also encouraged the team members to

LEAD AND SUCCEED

work together on complex situations, which led to more rapid learning and effective teamwork. The project was a success, and later in their careers, several of the team members went on to advanced degrees and careers in accounting—an unfamiliar field to them before working on the team.

USE QUESTIONS TO CREATE LEARNING MOMENTS

In Jesus's day, Capernaum was a fishing village on the north shore of the Sea of Galilee. Today the ruins of the synagogue referenced in this scripture are excavated and are one of the locations in Israel where we can be certain that Jesus walked.

> When they had come to Capernaum, those who received the temple tax came to Peter and said, "Does your Teacher not pay the temple tax?" He said, "Yes." And when he had come into the house, Jesus anticipated him, saying, "What do you think, Simon? From whom do the kings of the earth take customs or taxes, from their sons or from strangers?" Peter said to Him, "From strangers." Jesus said to him, "Then the sons are free. Nevertheless, lest we offend them, go to the sea, cast in a hook, and take the fish that comes up first. And when you have opened its mouth, you will find a piece of money; take that and give it to them for Me and you."
>
> —MATTHEW 17:24–27

Jesus customarily used daily situations as opportunities to teach and mentor His disciples. Jesus often threaded these "lessons" with pointed questions that reinforced the learning. In this situation, Jesus could have simply handled the need and modeled the expectations. Instead, He chose to give Peter some one-on-one coaching about what He was doing and why, and He used questions as His primary tool. When you engage people through questions that require an answer, you help them to listen actively. Also, when they answer correctly—even if you point them to the correct answer through additional questions—they feel good about themselves and are even more open to the mentoring. Use questions often, and you'll find people "get it" more readily.

152

Coach, Mentor, and Model

Live It

- Look for opportunities to teach and coach others—they exist in virtually any situation.

- Remember that questions are valuable, especially for confusing situations or when your actions could be misinterpreted without explanation.

- Craft a learning situation through questions.
    - Make sure the issue or situation is clear.
    - Ask broad questions—ones that require the other person to think before giving a response—because it will engage and cause him or her to think more deeply.
    - Express your views of the situation.

- As much as possible, allow the learner to be active in following through with the required action to reinforce the learning; note Jesus ensured the temple tax was paid and allowed Peter to take the action, thus reinforcing that God would provide.

See It

After reviewing fifty job applications and interviewing the top five candidates twice, the director of a publishing firm decided to hire a promising new designer right out of school.

The first day on the job, the director walked the new designer through a half-day orientation. At the end of the orientation, he introduced the designer to a senior designer who would lead his six-month training process. The new designer looked a bit offended. "I don't need six more months of training." The director agreed he graduated from a great school but explained, "They didn't teach you what you need to know for this job and our company."

A week later, the senior designer approached the director. "I can't get any work done. The new guy won't shut up. He's always asking questions." The director saw a learning moment and asked, "Has he asked the same question twice?" The senior designer thought for a moment and admitted he hadn't. Instantly he got it and went back to the training process with a renewed

153

LEAD AND SUCCEED

sense of purpose in his role. Eventually the two designers, both benefiting from learning moments based on questions, became best friends and won national awards together.

CAPITALIZE ON "TEACHABLE" MOMENTS

This scripture tells of Jesus healing a servant boy. It is notable in several ways. First, it is one of a few instances where Jesus is recorded as ministering to a non-Jew. Also, Jesus notes the centurion had "much faith"—perhaps the main reason He chose to use the situation to teach some deeper truths.

> Now when Jesus had entered Capernaum, a centurion came to Him, pleading with Him, saying, "Lord, my servant is lying at home paralyzed, dreadfully tormented." And Jesus said to him, "I will come and heal him." The centurion answered and said, "Lord, I am not worthy that You should come under my roof. But only speak a word, and my servant will be healed. For I also am a man under authority, having soldiers under me. And I say to this one, 'Go,' and he goes; and to another, 'Come,' and he comes; and to my servant, 'Do this,' and he does it." When Jesus heard it, He marveled, and said to those who followed, "Assuredly, I say to you, I have not found such great faith, not even in Israel! And I say to you that many will come from east and west, and sit down with Abraham, Isaac, and Jacob in the kingdom of heaven. But the sons of the kingdom will be cast out into outer darkness. There will be weeping and gnashing of teeth." Then Jesus said to the centurion, "Go your way; and as you have believed, so let it be done for you." And his servant was healed that same hour.
>
> —MATTHEW 8:5–13

The most effective leaders see themselves as teachers and mentors—helping others to reach their highest potential. With this mind-set, it is easier to take the time to use everyday situations as opportunities to develop others. In this instance, Jesus explained the significance of what

154

the centurion had said. He made it a priority to teach the people and not simply to take action. Consider how less meaningful this story would be if Jesus simply told the centurion to go and find his servant healed. Instead, His followers learned about authority and faith. In today's fast-paced work world, it is easy to prioritize the tasks over the people. Choose to be one of the leaders who prioritize "teachable" moments, and reap the benefits of a team that understands and acts on what they have learned from you.

Live It

- Check your mind-set.
    - Are you more concerned about getting your work done or about the people and how well they are positioned for producing results?
    - Do you prioritize learning on a regular basis?
    - What can you do to use everyday situations to help others see and understand what you are doing and why?
- Recognize the situations that are "ripe" for learning; for instance, when you...
    - Find yourself thinking through a number of important considerations—considerations others will benefit from knowing.
    - Think back on experiences you've had that others may not have—experiences you may not have shared yet.
    - See the opportunity to convey an important priority you want to emphasize—one that may not be fully evident or needs to be highlighted.
    - Know others will face the situation again in the future— and you can help them handle it themselves using your insights.
- Explain the learning first—then reinforce it by letting others watch you take action and participate as appropriate.

LEAD AND SUCCEED

See It

As both a consultant and leader, I've often stopped while working on something with others and called a "school" moment. "OK, this is Culture 401 school..." where the number indicates how advanced the topic is (equating to university level courses). During one such situation where I was leading consultants from another group, I needed to explain how to use a particular technique. When I called an advanced "school" moment, I was met with questions and comments from one consultant that indicated some of the fundamentals were missing—foundational understanding I assumed was there because of the consultant's role and level. So we stopped on the technique, and I went into the necessary basics—but chose not to embarrass her by giving it a low number! Not only was she eventually a success at using the advanced technique, but I had also gained an advocate for the work as we rolled out an innovation.

DEMONSTRATE A BALANCED WORK LIFE

Exodus describes the Israelites leaving Egypt for the Promised Land. It also contains the Ten Commandments and other laws for the people to follow, such as this section that augments the commandment concerning the Sabbath, or day of rest.

> Six years you shall sow your land and gather in its produce, but the seventh year you shall let it rest and lie fallow, that the poor of your people may eat; and what they leave, the beasts of the field may eat. In like manner you shall do with your vineyard and your olive grove. Six days you shall do your work, and on the seventh day you shall rest, that your ox and your donkey may rest, and the son of your female servant and the stranger may be refreshed.
>
> —Exodus 23:10–12

Your work habits directly impact others as an example of what they should do. In fact, some may believe they *must* follow your work habits to be successful or seen as doing "enough." If you overwork yourself, you are risking problems with your own quality, productivity, and health, and you

156

Coach, Mentor, and Model

are also sending not-so-subtle signals for others to do the same. God set aside a day for rest—and extended it to all key means of business in that day, including workers, land, and other resources. If you maintain reasonable limits on your own work life, it will benefit you as well as the people who work for you in quality and productivity—and in morale and attitude.

Live It

- Recognize people listen to what you say, but what you do will always "speak" much more loudly.

- Remember God has set a clear "one-day-in-seven" expectation for us to follow, and today's business requirements should not be made an excuse for pushing yourself or others to overwork.

- Acknowledge adequate rest and recreation are essential to be effective at work, and that a properly rested person is more likely to produce quality work in less time and experience fewer absences.

- Set aside a regular day for worship, family, and rest—and resist the temptation to let work slip into that day.

- Remember your work will never "be done"; you'll continually need to prioritize things and let some less important things drop or wait.

See It

One division found its new top executive had set a problematic pattern for the organization. An admitted "workaholic," this executive regularly started his day two or three hours before "normal" business hours, worked well into the nights, and even kept long hours on the weekends. He was also "hands-on"—someone who wanted to know the details of the work and answers "right now." Although the division was dispersed geographically, they kept in touch with each other through e-mail and instant messages, as well as regular calls and periodic face-to-face meetings. The top executive regularly sent messages to people across the organization during his extended

LEAD AND SUCCEED

working hours and then became noticeably frustrated when others did not answer within a short time, even outside normal business hours.

Eventually the leaders reporting to this executive found themselves constantly checking messages—and they also began to emulate the same pattern of off-hour communication expectations with their staffs. The division soon found its morale dropping, employee turnover climbing, and customer satisfaction scores falling. The illusion of higher productivity from more hours had taken a toll on the organization and its effectiveness. Ultimately the division required senior leader changes along with external consulting help to turn things around.

CONCLUSION

Business leaders who prioritize others by making regular time to coach and mentor them—and model expectations—are depositing valuable nuggets into their lives. All of us can point to people who took the time to make a difference—and often it was only a small effort that became so valuable for us. Aspire to be a "net giver" as a leader in business, using the Bible for examples on how to guide others.

chapter twelve

DEVELOP EFFECTIVE TEAMS

Increase collective results by enabling others to work well together

L EADERS ARE RESPONSIBLE for many tasks, and enabling others to do their work well together is one of the basics. In fact, as mentioned earlier, a leader's effectiveness can best be seen by what happens when he or she is absent. Leaders who fail to develop teams are simply technicians in the wrong position. Even if you must admit you've functioned as more of a technician than a leader in the past, it's never too late to grow in this important area. The Bible provides examples of what to do and how to do it. In particular, it shows how Jesus worked to create a team from the twelve disciples—a team whose work impacted the entire world.

ENSURE TEAMS HAVE NEEDED LEADERSHIP

After taking the Promised Land, the Israelites went through a period of several hundred years before the monarchy was established with Saul as the first king. This time is documented in the Book of Judges. Over and over, the Israelites demonstrated the importance of leadership and how easily people can get off track without it.

> And they were left, that He might test Israel by them, to know whether they would obey the commandments of the LORD, which He had commanded their fathers by the hand of Moses.
>
> Thus the children of Israel dwelt among the Canaanites, the Hittites, the Amorites, the Perizzites, the Hivites, and the Jebusites. And they took their daughters to be their

LEAD AND SUCCEED

wives, and gave their daughters to their sons; and they
served their gods.

So the children of Israel did evil in the sight of the
LORD. They forgot the LORD their God, and served the
Baals and Asherahs. Therefore the anger of the LORD
was hot against Israel, and He sold them into the hand
of Cushan-Rishathaim king of Mesopotamia; and the
children of Israel served Cushan-Rishathaim eight years.
When the children of Israel cried out to the LORD, the
LORD raised up a deliverer for the children of Israel, who
delivered them: Othniel the son of Kenaz, Caleb's younger
brother. The Spirit of the LORD came upon him, and he
judged Israel. He went out to war, and the LORD delivered Cushan-Rishathaim king of Mesopotamia into his
hand; and his hand prevailed over Cushan-Rishathaim. So
the land had rest for forty years. Then Othniel the son of
Kenaz died.

And the children of Israel again did evil in the sight of
the LORD. So the LORD strengthened Eglon king of Moab
against Israel, because they had done evil in the sight of the
LORD....

In those days there was no king in Israel; everyone did
what was right in his own eyes.

—JUDGES 3:4–12; 17:6

These verses indicate the importance of leadership for any group of
people—extending to departments and work teams in business. Teams can
function with varying degrees of autonomy, but direction and oversight
are critical to ensure teams stay on track with their responsibilities. When
you establish clear boundaries of responsibility for the team—and monitor
and reinforce them to ensure the requirements are met—you are creating
an environment for an effective team and for satisfied team members. It is
important to note this responsibility never goes away even when a team has
been effective for a period of time. As the above scriptures indicate, even
good performance can deteriorate quickly without the right maintenance.

160

Develop Effective Teams

Live It

- Recognize that leading teams takes a balance: directing people by establishing boundaries and giving direction, and letting the team have the freedom to execute their work and develop their own way of working together.

- Remember that effective teams focus on both tasks and relationships—on what they do and how they do it.

- Resist the temptation to get too involved in directing *how* the team should work—and focus instead on *what* they need to accomplish and what resources they need to achieve it.

- Determine the type of leadership appropriate for the team's capability.
    - Early in a team's development, people need clear direction, and they may also need detailed guidance, knowledge, and skills.
    - Shortly into a team's development, it is inevitable for some "storming"—or team conflict—to occur; expect it, tell people it is normal, and be ready to help them through the issues if they go on too long.
    - As teams develop their own capabilities and begin to produce consistent results, the leader should ensure the team has the needed autonomy to act, yet be available to help resolve issues they may face.

- Maintain your leadership role over time, adjusting for the team's effectiveness and giving them appropriate degrees of autonomy while continuing to ensure they stay on track.

See It

"This is a team of leaders. They'll find a way to be successful." I heard the words, but I still felt concerned about a warning sign that led me to speak with a client's executive. I had been asked to run a teaming exercise to launch a new team, and some of the participants did poorly on it. They

LEAD AND SUCCEED

argued about the approach they would use in doing the exercise together and, as a consequence, did not fulfill the exercise requirements. I had seen it before—and knew it could mean trouble. I felt the team needed careful leadership, especially as they started up, because they were off to a rocky start. Because the team's charter was clear—and the team contained a number of successful leaders—the executive wasn't too concerned about the issue I raised, so he left them alone to do their work. I trusted his judgment, knowing he knew the people and I didn't.

So I went back to my "regular" consulting work for that client and forgot about the concerns. Unfortunately, I heard the team fell apart a short time later. The issues that plagued them during the exercise continued—and because the executive adopted a hands-off approach, they lacked the leadership they needed. The important work was delayed, and a new team had to be assembled to complete it. This time, the executive was more engaged and the project succeeded.

GUIDE TEAMS BY ESTABLISHING THE BASICS OF THEIR MISSION

During Jesus's three-year ministry, He empowered the twelve disciples to cast out demons and cure diseases—a task He expected them to accomplish on their own without Him. Matthew 10:1 through 11:1 provides leaders with the perfect example of what Jesus did to provide the needed information and support to get His team started on their task. The key verses are covered in the next four sections, but consider the entire passage as a manual on how to charter a team.

> And when He had called His twelve disciples to Him, He gave them power over unclean spirits, to cast them out, and to heal all kinds of sickness and all kinds of disease....
> These twelve Jesus sent out and commanded them, saying: "Do not go into the way of the Gentiles, and do not enter a city of the Samaritans. But go rather to the lost sheep of the house of Israel. And as you go, preach, saying, 'The kingdom of heaven is at hand.' Heal the sick, cleanse the lepers, raise the dead, cast out demons. Freely you have received, freely

162

Develop Effective Teams

give. Provide neither gold nor silver nor copper in your money belts, nor bag for your journey, nor two tunics, nor sandals, nor staffs; for a worker is worthy of his food."
—Matthew 10:1, 5–10

Here, Jesus succinctly lays out all of the elements teams need to know to be prepared for their responsibilities. He specified who was on the team, authority given and results expected, scope of the work (what it did and did not include), important messages to deliver, specific tasks to accomplish, the way or "style" to conduct the work, and finally the resources and their source. Not only are these the vital elements needed when launching a team, but they are also valuable to reinforce throughout the team's work and can help uncover the reasons when a team is floundering. Return to this passage every time you launch a new team and follow Jesus's example. It will greatly enhance the success of the team.

Live It

- Recognize it is easy to assume teams understand what they need to be successful—and dedicate yourself to carefully clarifying each element every time you launch a team.

- Be sure you provide clear answers to the questions the team will ask directly or assume if you don't clarify.
    - What results do you expect and when?
    - Who are the members of the team, and who will lead the team? How will you personally be involved?
    - What authority does the team have to make decisions, take action, and address issues?
    - What is the scope for the work? What do you want the team not to do that they may assume is part of their charter?
    - Are there important messages, tasks, or approaches to the work you want the team to prioritize?
    - What resources will be made available?

LEAD AND SUCCEED

- If you are a team member and the leader has not clarified some of the above elements, be sure to ask questions and not simply assume the answers!

- Recognize that the ordering of the elements may be important—and Jesus provided a perfect example for us to follow.

- Clarify the answers to these questions as the team launches its work, and reinforce them periodically.

See It

One team found out the hard way that being proactive about their charter may be necessary when the leader has not done it. Their company needed to implement a shared service capability to improve the sales process. The senior executive responsible for implementing the capability identified the key leaders for the team, the results he expected from them, the scope of the functions, and territories to be included. He even gave the team broad decision authority to get the job done. But the executive didn't discuss what resources would be made available—and the team assumed they would get the funding and people they needed because it was such an important project.

After two weeks of intensive planning, the team came forward with a detailed, doable plan that included when the capability could be up and running. But when the team discussed what it would take to support the plan, the senior executive informed them they could expect only about half of their plan's assumptions for funding and people. The team explained they would need to revise their plans, especially the dates the capabilities would be functional. Unfortunately, the original dates were now cemented in the executive's expectations—and the team was told to "go make it happen." The team felt "stuck" and that the senior executive's expectations were unreasonable.

Given their charge, they felt they had no other option but to go back and cut corners on key activities they believed were necessary for success. In other words, the only change open to them was to reduce the quality of their work. They grudgingly selected certain work they would not do. The team

164

met their dates and budgets, so the senior executive was initially pleased. However, as the shared service was rolled out, the team's work was not seen as successful. The organization struggled to implement a design that was not fully complete and had not adequately considered the organizational implications. The needed adjustments were made over time, but members of the team felt their reputations had been negatively impacted by the project.

PREPARE TEAMS FOR POSSIBLE OPPOSITION

Jesus and His disciples were continually on the move from town to town ministering and preaching to the people. In this second of four sections about chartering teams, Jesus prepared the disciples for the reactions they would face in the assignment He was giving them.

Now whatever city or town you enter, inquire who in it is worthy, and stay there till you go out. And when you go into a household, greet it. If the household is worthy, let your peace come upon it. But if it is not worthy, let your peace return to you. And whoever will not receive you nor hear your words, when you depart from that house or city, shake off the dust from your feet. Assuredly, I say to you, it will be more tolerable for the land of Sodom and Gomorrah in the day of judgment than for that city!

Behold, I send you out as sheep in the midst of wolves. Therefore be wise as serpents and harmless as doves. But beware of men, for they will deliver you up to councils and scourge you in their synagogues. You will be brought before governors and kings for My sake, as a testimony to them and to the Gentiles. But when they deliver you up, do not worry about how or what you should speak. For it will be given to you in that hour what you should speak; for it is not you who speak, but the Spirit of your Father who speaks in you. Now brother will deliver up brother to death, and a father his child; and children will rise up against parents and cause them to be put to death. And you will be hated by all for My name's sake. But he who endures to the end will be

LEAD AND SUCCEED

saved. When they persecute you in this city, flee to another. For assuredly, I say to you, you will not have gone through the cities of Israel before the Son of Man comes....

Are not two sparrows sold for a copper coin? And not one of them falls to the ground apart from your Father's will. But the very hairs of your head are all numbered. Do not fear therefore; you are of more value than many sparrows.
—MATTHEW 10:11–23, 29–31

In great depth, Jesus explained to the disciples the opposition they were likely to face. He also told them why: because they were representing Him. Teams will often face opposition because it is a natural consequence of change—the exact reason many teams are launched. Jesus also told His team where they would receive help for that opposition: from the Holy Spirit for what to say and from the Father as overall "sponsor" for their work. When you launch a new team, anticipate the possible opposition the team may face and prepare the members for it. You will help the team members understand the difficulties of their work and know what to do—and not feel as if they have done something wrong to cause it. As always, Jesus provides a perfect example of how to do this.

Live It

+ Be realistic with yourself and your teams about the potential for resistance and opposition.

+ Provide teams with any history they'll need to understand possible reactions; without it, they may make some problems worse despite good intentions.

+ Give guidance on how they may be able to readily recognize the opposition or resistance; sometimes it can be subtle, so they'll function best if they know what you know about it.

+ Clarify your expectations, including how you want the team to respond—what they should and should not say and do.

Develop Effective Teams

- Reinforce your support for the team's work, and clarify how you will actively engage as needed to help them overcome the issues they face.

See It

"Frankly, I wouldn't be surprised if you've given up in six weeks." Not exactly the welcome I expected when I joined an especially difficult project that had been underway for months. I was sitting with the project executive, who was openly going over the history of the project and the client and how my two predecessors had quit the project, claiming the organizational change risks were impossible to resolve. The client had failed multiple times at the same effort, even with other consultants helping them, and a great skepticism permeated the organization. This troubled history just added to the general resistance to the project's requirements and its implications.

The project executive's candid discussion of the issues caused me to ask many questions—and to choose certain ways to approach the work. Most important was the need to convince the project executive that I would only take action she believed was best. After several iterations of frustrating analysis and planning that were met with "no" when I sought approval to proceed, we finally agreed on a path to overcome the opposition (which, by the way, was my primary reason for being on the project). The approach proved successful, and we succeeded in helping the client finally reach its goal. Had I pushed forward without understanding the history and opposition, I would have approached the project in a very different way and probably compounded the problems. Instead, we had a happy client and were able to boast a success our competitors had not achieved!

ENSURE THE TEAM KNOWS YOUR EXPECTATIONS AND THE REWARDS

The Gospels of Mark and Luke also record Jesus chartering the disciples, but the accounts are less detailed. (See Mark 6:7–13 and Luke 9:1–6.) Matthew's account provides additional detail about Jesus's expectations for the disciples—information vital to both their immediate role in ministering to the people and to their longer-term role as initial leaders of the

Christian church. These expectations make up the third aspect of the disciples' charter.

> Therefore whoever confesses Me before men, him I will also confess before My Father who is in heaven. But whoever denies Me before men, him I will also deny before My Father who is in heaven....
>
> And he who does not take his cross and follow after Me is not worthy of Me. He who finds his life will lose it, and he who loses his life for My sake will find it.
>
> He who receives you receives Me, and he who receives Me receives Him who sent Me. He who receives a prophet in the name of a prophet shall receive a prophet's reward. And he who receives a righteous man in the name of a righteous man shall receive a righteous man's reward. And whoever gives one of these little ones only a cup of cold water in the name of a disciple, assuredly, I say to you, he shall by no means lose his reward.
>
> —MATTHEW 10:32, 38–42

While instructing His disciples, Jesus clarified His expectations. Notice He stated what He wanted and did not want, along with the associated positive and negative consequences. Jesus encouraged the team to follow His example of the actions to take—another expectation, and one all leaders should aspire to be in a position to do! Make sure your team clearly understands your expectations and the rewards they can expect from it. It will propel them quickly toward achieving the work.

Live It

- Always aspire to be a good example—one you can encourage others to follow to achieve the expectations you set for them.

- Remember to reinforce your core expectations—and launching a team is a great time because you have everyone's attention.

Develop Effective Teams

- Craft the message to communicate your expectations.
  - State what you want—and do not want—people to do.
  - Emphasize the reasons these expectations are important.
  - Indicate the consequences, both the positive ones when people meet the expectations and the negative ones when they do not.
  - Clarify any special circumstances or challenges the team may face and how they relate to your expectations.
- Deliver the message, and redeliver it over time to reinforce your expectations and ensure people stay on track and motivated for the work.

See It

"This is the most transformational program this company has undertaken in a very long time," the sponsor told his team at the program's kickoff. "I need each of you to put down your organizational silos and design what will be best for our company as a whole." With those words, the executive clearly signaled to members of his team this program would be different from others. "I want you to know this program will be a real challenge for all of us because we must overcome a number of historic issues—and our culture is going to make it difficult for us."

His expectations were clear: the team needed to focus on the bigger picture and recognize that parts of their designs may be unpopular with their home departments. In later design reviews, the sponsor pressed the team with questions to ensure they were indeed considering the bigger picture—and how the customers, employees, and company would be better for it. Early on, the executive communicated his own personal motivation for the program: to leave a legacy at the company. He encouraged others to adopt the same mind-set—to build something lasting and be a part of the company's history. The executive went further to ensure the program had high visibility and provided lots of positive feedback and open recognition to members of the team. He also positioned many of the team members for the career advancement they sought. Over time, the program had a positive impact on the company, and the employees who participated in it were

LEAD AND SUCCEED

proud of their contributions and rewarded in many ways for having done an important piece of work.

WHEN THE TEAM IS READY, GET OUT OF THE WAY

This is the last of four sections devoted to Jesus chartering the disciples to take action on His behalf from Matthew 10:1 through 11:1. Before this final verse, Jesus had communicated all the instructions the disciples needed, along with information to motivate them to fulfill the instructions.

> Now it came to pass, when Jesus finished commanding His twelve disciples, that He departed from there to teach and to preach in their cities.
>
> —MATTHEW 11:1

Having provided the needed instructions, Jesus sent the disciples on their way to complete their work while He went on to do other things. This sentence makes an important point: He did not micromanage their work. Jesus had given them enough instruction so He could expect them to use their best judgment to carry out the details. This was the opportunity for the disciples to learn by doing, bounded by thorough charter He had provided in Matthew 10. By getting out of the way, Jesus demonstrated He trusted the disciples to fulfill His expectations and encouraged them to think for themselves and handle the circumstances they faced. When you follow the pattern of chartering people and teams found in Matthew 10—and the vital point of Matthew 11:1 about getting out of the way—you help teams to grow and produce great results. The entire process provides people with the needed instructions, boundaries, and appropriate latitude for executing the work, along with multiple reasons for feeling good about their accomplishments.

Live It

- Remember a leader's impact is best demonstrated when he or she is not there—when people are fulfilling their responsibilities within the set boundaries.

Develop Effective Teams

- Verify people understand your expectations and what they should do—then allow them to take action.

- Determine the proper degree of oversight and involvement depending on the team's capabilities—and recognize it is frequently best to start with less oversight so you can more easily determine what they can do on their own.

- Be cognizant that it is easy to be too close to the team's work (micromanagement) and too distant (absentee leader), and that you need to seek the right balance in each situation.

See It

One team was venting its frustration. "Not only is this work not using my capabilities, but also I'm sick of the endless reviews that cause low-value, time-consuming changes."

Another member nodded. "We have such a great team, but the manager is ruining it with how she handles us. I've never been so micromanaged in my entire career." The manager had handpicked the "dream team"—people with the expertise needed to do a stellar job on a difficult project. But her own style was getting in the way of success. She was admittedly "hands-on" and liked to be part of the details. But this was causing frustration among team members who wanted—and expected—latitude to get the work done. Instead, they faced constant rework due to the manager's frequent reviews.

Eventually, the team began to devise ways to delay reviews until they were ready for the detailed work that would come after them. They also went through elaborate planning on how to accomplish each delay. The team was successful in meeting many of the goals set for it, but the manager's style led several key people to transfer out of the group. Also, her reputation made it difficult to hire new people at the same caliber to replace them. In their new jobs, many of the people stayed in touch with one another and reminisced about how things could have been better—and how the "dream team" might have stayed together under a different manager.

LEAD AND SUCCEED

CONCLUSION

The Bible provides a number of examples for developing teams, especially through Jesus and His work with the twelve disciples. Return to this chapter when you are launching a new team or when you sense a team is struggling. It will help you know the Bible's wisdom for leading others to achieve effective results together.

chapter thirteen

CORRECT PEOPLE COMPASSIONATELY
Address failures with a balance on relationships and results

ORRECTING PEOPLE IS a necessary, although difficult, requirement for leaders. Correcting people the right way can increase productivity and morale. Correcting them the wrong way, however, can lead to ongoing issues with both relationships and results. The Bible shows leaders how to be both firm and merciful at the same time. Follow these examples, and you will be neither a wimp nor a tyrant in how you handle people when they need correction.

CORRECT WITH AN EYE ON THE FUTURE

Hebrews is a letter written to New Testament Jewish believers. Chapter 12 of Hebrews covers the important topic of giving and receiving correction.

> And you have forgotten the exhortation which speaks to you as to sons: "My son, do not despise the chastening of the LORD, nor be discouraged when you are rebuked by Him; for whom the LORD loves He chastens, and scourges every son whom He receives."
>
> If you endure chastening, God deals with you as with sons; for what son is there whom a father does not chasten? But if you are without chastening, of which all have become partakers, then you are illegitimate and not sons. Furthermore, we have had human fathers who corrected us, and we paid them respect. Shall we not much more readily be in subjection to the Father of spirits and live? For they indeed for a few days chastened us as seemed best to them, but

LEAD AND SUCCEED

He for our profit, that we may be partakers of His holiness.
Now no chastening seems to be joyful for the present, but
painful; nevertheless, afterward it yields the peaceable fruit
of righteousness to those who have been trained by it.

—HEBREWS 12:5–11

It is difficult to correct others and natural to want to avoid confrontation
and its backlash. Certainly, no one enjoys being corrected, and many people
respond by becoming defensive, hostile, sullen, or depressed. But leaders
need to put this into proper perspective. If we fail to give a deserved correction to someone due to fear of a negative reaction, then we are dodging a key
responsibility of leadership. Conversely, we should always be ready to accept
correction by those in authority over us. Choose to see correction—both
giving and receiving it—as a necessary part of business life and a way for you
to show respect for people and their long-term capabilities.

Live It

- Acknowledge correcting people is an ongoing responsibility
  of leadership.

- Check your motivation, and if you are correcting without
  genuine concern for a person's future, you need to examine
  what you are doing and why.

- Check your emotions, and if you are overly emotional (for
  example, angry), use prayer to get yourself under control
  before taking action.

- Acknowledge that giving correction is uncomfortable, and
  resist the temptation to wait, thinking it will be easier later.

- Select the appropriate time to give correction—looking for a
  time when the recipient is most ready to receive it and has a
  chance to work through his or her own reactions.

- Choose the place for correction, preferably somewhere
  private, and remember to remove distractions by turning off

174

Correct People Compassionately

your phone, closing your door, and making sure you won't be disturbed.

- Identify the problem and ask questions to give the person ample opportunity to give their perspective on what happened and why—and be willing to change your perspective about the situation if warranted.

- Ask the person to repeat back your expectations—being sure to listen carefully and to clarify any misunderstandings.
    - Often during correction, people fail to listen effectively due to emotions, so be patient and repeat your expectations several times if necessary.

- Set a time to follow up and review performance—being available to support the person's progress but avoiding the temptation to be too active in the work he or she must do.

- Set a good example by constructively handling situations where you need to accept correction; it will increase your credibility and compassion.

See It

Early in my career, I was brought in to lead an intact department. Soon I discovered a member of the team who produced significantly more errors than others. In dealing with the situation, I followed most of the "live it" steps but failed in one of them. By focusing too strongly on the needed performance and ensuring he had the needed knowledge and skills, I neglected to ask questions to uncover his thinking about the work and the errors he made. Only much later in a long, difficult process did I come to realize we had different mind-sets about the importance of accuracy. Had I opened a dialogue through questions to get his perspective, I believe the situation could have been easier and more successful for both of us.

175

LEAD AND SUCCEED

SURFACE CONFESSIONS ABOUT FAILURES AND MISTAKES

Genesis opens with God's creation of the heavens and earth and His initial dealings with humankind. Adam and Eve lived in the idyllic Garden of Eden where there were only a few rules to follow—one of which they broke. Genesis 3 tells the story of their failure and how God dealt with it.

Then the LORD God took the man and put him in the garden of Eden to tend and keep it. And the LORD God commanded the man, saying, "Of every tree of the garden you may freely eat; but of the tree of the knowledge of good and evil you shall not eat, for in the day that you eat of it you shall surely die."...

So when the woman saw that the tree was good for food, that it was pleasant to the eyes, and a tree desirable to make one wise, she took of its fruit and ate. She also gave to her husband with her, and he ate. Then the eyes of both of them were opened, and they knew that they were naked; and they sewed fig leaves together and made themselves coverings. And they heard the sound of the LORD God walking in the garden in the cool of the day, and Adam and his wife hid themselves from the presence of the LORD God among the trees of the garden.

Then the LORD God called to Adam and said to him, "Where are you?" So he said, "I heard Your voice in the garden, and I was afraid because I was naked; and I hid myself." And He said, "Who told you that you were naked? Have you eaten from the tree of which I commanded you that you should not eat?" Then the man said, "The woman whom You gave to be with me, she gave me of the tree, and I ate." And the LORD God said to the woman, "What is this you have done?" The woman said, "The serpent deceived me, and I ate."...

176

Correct People Compassionately

To the woman He said: "I will greatly multiply your sorrow and your conception; in pain you shall bring forth children; your desire shall be for your husband, and he shall rule over you."

Then to Adam He said, "Because you have heeded the voice of your wife, and have eaten from the tree of which I commanded you, saying, 'You shall not eat of it': Cursed is the ground for your sake; in toil you shall eat of it all the days of your life. Both thorns and thistles it shall bring forth for you, and you shall eat the herb of the field. In the sweat of your face you shall eat bread till you return to the ground, for out of it you were taken; for dust you are, and to dust you shall return."...

Also for Adam and his wife the LORD God made tunics of skin, and clothed them.... Therefore the LORD God sent him out of the garden of Eden to till the ground from which he was taken.

—GENESIS 2:15–17; 3:6–13, 16–19, 21, 23

Ever wonder why the all-knowing God questioned Adam and Eve about their transgression? He *knew* what had happened, so why didn't He just tell them what was *going* to happen as a result? He chose instead to ask questions to begin the process of accountability, consequences, and restoration.

When problems arise, leaders should begin with questions to solicit input and confessions from those involved. When you hand out consequences based on admissions of guilt, they are more likely to be accepted as appropriate. Also note Adam and Eve received different consequences. Discipline needs to be appropriate to a person's particular part in the problem or failure. Follow God's example, and experience more effective results when you must correct someone.

LEAD AND SUCCEED

Live It

- Establish clear "dos" and "don'ts" for each situation—and for important requirements, identify the consequences for noncompliance in advance.

- Stay close enough to be aware of changes in how people respond to you; it may signal a problem.

- When noncompliance is evident, use questions to ensure your understanding of the problem and identify people's specific involvement.

- Allow each person to admit what he or she did to enhance your knowledge of the situation, and help them accept the consequences.

- Assign consequences based on what each person did.

- Consider whether some negative aspects should be mitigated for both the sake of relationships and for how others will perceive the situation; for example, the tunics God made for Adam and Eve reduced some negative aspects of their punishment yet kept the punishment intact.

- Adopt a long-term view of the situation and ensure your actions address both the immediate problem and any likely future implications.

See It

A senior executive faced a particularly sticky issue with an heir apparent for one of his organizations. The man had just publicly displayed insubordination toward that organization's current manager—someone the senior executive intended to remove shortly. His first inclination was to move forward with his plan and promote the offender. However, the executive realized this action would "reward," or at least ignore, the unacceptable behavior. If he moved ahead with the promotion, it might encourage others to follow suit. So the executive met with the offender and used questions to uncover the man's view of the situation. He admitted his actions were wrong but felt they were justi-

Correct People Compassionately

fied given the manager's incompetence. The executive then announced his decision: he was going to transfer the man to an unfavorable department, and he would also be ineligible for the soon-to-be-open top position. However, the transfer would be only for one year, and additional promotion opportunities were expected after he returned. The consequences were severe yet measured in terms of the man's long-term career with the company. By his decision, and the way he handled the interaction, the senior executive sent a strong message to the organization about his expectations.

ADDRESS UNACKNOWLEDGED FAILURES AND MISTAKES

Adam and Eve had children after they were banished from the Garden of Eden. Two of their sons, Cain and Abel, were participants in the world's first murder.

And in the process of time it came to pass that Cain brought an offering of the fruit of the ground to the LORD. Abel also brought of the firstborn of his flock and of their fat. And the LORD respected Abel and his offering, but He did not respect Cain and his offering. And Cain was very angry, and his countenance fell. So the LORD said to Cain, "Why are you angry? And why has your countenance fallen? If you do well, will you not be accepted? And if you do not do well, sin lies at the door. And its desire is for you, but you should rule over it." Now Cain talked with Abel his brother; and it came to pass, when they were in the field, that Cain rose up against Abel his brother and killed him.

Then the LORD said to Cain, "Where is Abel your brother?" He said, "I do not know. Am I my brother's keeper?" And He said, "What have you done? The voice of your brother's blood cries out to Me from the ground. So now you are cursed from the earth, which has opened its mouth to receive your brother's blood from your hand. When you till the ground, it shall no longer yield its strength to you. A fugitive and a vagabond you shall be on the earth." And Cain said to the

179

LEAD AND SUCCEED

LORD, "My punishment is greater than I can bear! Surely You have driven me out this day from the face of the ground; I shall be hidden from Your face; I shall be a fugitive and a vagabond on the earth, and it will happen that anyone who finds me will kill me." And the LORD said to him, "Therefore, whoever kills Cain, vengeance shall be taken on him sevenfold." And the LORD set a mark on Cain, lest anyone finding him should kill him.

Then Cain went out from the presence of the LORD and dwelt in the land of Nod on the east of Eden.

—GENESIS 4:3–16

Cain and Abel both knew how to make an offering. Otherwise, God would have instructed Cain rather than remind him to follow the proper method. But Cain chose not to do what he knew was right. When a person deliberately does not do what is required, it is often evidenced by a growing pattern. For this reason, it is best to address the first failure firmly—even if seems to be a small one—because it may prevent more serious problems. Cain's first failure, not following a known procedure, led to a very serious sin: murder. In confronting Cain, God used questions to seek an admission of guilt—then clarified the wrongdoing and assigned an appropriate consequence despite Cain's lack of confession. He also demonstrated the way to mitigate the negative aspects of a punishment without changing the punishment itself. It is easy to regret taking difficult actions with people, and this causes some leaders to later remove the punishment. Choose to be a leader who knows how to show firmness yet compassion by keeping the consequence intact and appropriately mitigating some of the negative aspects.

Live It

- Ensure the requirements of each assignment are clear and understood.

- Look for early warning signs, such as discontent and avoidance, and talk with the person to understand the issue and prevent future problems.

Correct People Compassionately

- When noncompliance is evident, use questions to explore the person's understanding of what he or she did wrong—and give the person a chance to admit the wrong.

- If the person will not admit it—and you know you have the facts straight—don't hesitate to take action, carefully communicating the failure and its consequences.

- Listen to the person's response, but avoid the temptation to minimize the failure or reduce appropriate consequences.

- If you learn new facts during the conversation, independently confirm the facts and decide if the consequences need to be modified.

- Consider the long-term impact of the consequence and mitigate negative fallout if appropriate.

See It

One company found out the hard way the result of dealing with failures too harshly. Over the years, an inappropriate "zero defects" philosophy had morphed into a style of leadership that handled even innocent mistakes with serious, visible reprimands and consequences. When one employee discovered a serious mistake, she was panic-stricken and sought to hide her mistake. But it only cost the company more, ultimately resulting in a loss of approximately $40,000 for the small company. The employee was fired, and more fear was created. The leaders realized they needed to change their approach. A policy was communicated: employees who immediately brought their honest mistakes to management would not be fired. Their resolve was quickly tested. Another costly mistake was soon made, but this time the employee brought it to their attention as soon as it was discovered. The leaders had to resist the urge to fire the employee, but in doing so, they initiated a new, less fearful environment within the company.

LEAD AND SUCCEED

BE ALERT FOR INCORRECT MIND-SETS

This incident occurred after Jesus's disciples had significant and repeated experiences with His powerful teaching and miracles. By this time, Jesus expected a greater level of understanding than His disciples displayed.

> And He left them, and getting into the boat again, departed to the other side. Now the disciples had forgotten to take bread, and they did not have more than one loaf with them in the boat. Then He charged them, saying, "Take heed, beware of the leaven of the Pharisees and the leaven of Herod." And they reasoned among themselves, saying, "It is because we have no bread." But Jesus, being aware of it, said to them, "Why do you reason because you have no bread? Do you not yet perceive nor understand? Is your heart still hardened? Having eyes, do you not see? And having ears, do you not hear? And do you not remember? When I broke the five loaves for the five thousand, how many baskets full of fragments did you take up?" They said to Him, "Twelve." "And when I broke the seven for the four thousand, how many large baskets full of fragments did you take up?" And they said, "Seven." So He said to them, "How is it you do not understand?"
>
> —MARK 8:13–21

The disciples should have had a better understanding than they demonstrated in this situation. Jesus corrected them, but He did it expressly so they would have improved understanding in the future. Rather than simply telling them what they should have already understood, He used pointed questions to get their attention and direct them to what they were missing. Engaging them in this manner got their attention and made it more likely they would retain the necessary lesson.

182

Correct People Compassionately

Live It

- Recognize the importance of mind-sets and how thinking impacts action.

- Address incorrect thoughts with the same passion as incorrect actions.

- Evaluate the level of understanding that should be expected.
  - If the person is relatively new to the responsibilities, point out the differences between correct and incorrect thinking.
  - If the person is growing in knowledge and ability, use open questions (for example, beginning with "what if" and "when") to direct the person's thinking toward areas of needed change.
  - If the person has had adequate time and support to understand, ask pointed questions to get attention and indicate areas needing correction.

- Focus on the person's long-term learning and overall success as your primary goals.

See It

One army unit was conducting a "paper exercise"—which involves detailed plans but no actual troops in the field. As each group submitted their plans, one of the headquarters leaders discovered a plan destined for failure. He started to alert the group to their error, but the colonel stopped him. "We'll shoot their helicopters down, and they will learn. Let them make this mistake when it doesn't cost any lives." The other leader had an incorrect mind-set about the paper exercises and what they were designed to do. Ensuring he understood the purpose of these exercises and handled them correctly would be vital to the overall effectiveness, and safety, of the unit in live combat.

183

LEAD AND SUCCEED

CONSIDER THE IMPACT OF A PUBLIC CORRECTION

This New Testament passage comes from a letter Paul wrote to his protégé Timothy. In it, Paul gives the young man instructions for church leadership.

> Those who are sinning rebuke in the presence of all, that the rest also may fear.
>
> —1 TIMOTHY 5:20

In general, leaders should talk to people one-on-one to discuss performance shortfalls. However, this passage refers to the motivational value of "learning another's lesson." If a problem is out in the open, it may be appropriate to correct publicly to ensure others are warned from the same path. If intentions were good and the person is noticeably aware of their shortfall, a private or mild open correction may be sufficient. Be sure to think beyond the immediate needs to the resulting impact on others before deciding the best course of action.

Live It

- Realize that people generally know the performance of others.

- Evaluate whether the performance failure was due to inexperience, honest mistakes, or if the person knew better and is capable of more.

- Choose the best way to address the situation, balancing the needs to correct the individual and send a clear message about your expectations.
  - Give a private, mild correction if the person is aware and sorry for his or her failure.
  - Give a private correction followed by a broader message about your expectations if others may be inclined to make the same mistake.
  - Give an open correction if the failure was open and serious.

See It

One organization found itself in the awkward place of having to try again to implement changes to its IT processes and procedures. Several previous attempts had failed, yet the improvements were necessary. When the new attempt was announced, many openly scoffed, but most people simply ignored the message. To get attention, the project team implemented an open measurement system. The key requirements were identified along with expected standards and timing for completion. Project members met regularly with leaders of the organization to go over their group's performance against expectations, and all were repeatedly alerted that results would be openly published in an upcoming meeting. The meeting came and went, and the inadequate performance of several groups was known to all—as was the superior performance of others. By the next meeting, all results were at or above expectations, and soon the effort was well on its way to success.

ENSURE NEGATIVE CONSEQUENCES ARE FIRM

Moses is the person speaking to God in this passage. This episode happened shortly before his death. Moses was not permitted to enter the Promised Land due to a serious sin he committed. (See Numbers 20:2–13.)

> Then I pleaded with the LORD at that time, saying: "O Lord GOD, You have begun to show Your servant Your greatness and Your mighty hand, for what god is there in heaven or on earth who can do anything like Your works and Your mighty deeds? I pray, let me cross over and see the good land beyond the Jordan, those pleasant mountains, and Lebanon." But the LORD was angry with me on your account, and would not listen to me. So the LORD said to me: "Enough of that! Speak no more to Me of this matter. Go up to the top of Pisgah, and lift your eyes toward the west, the north, the south, and the east; behold it with your eyes, for you shall not cross over this Jordan. But command Joshua, and encourage him and strengthen him; for he shall go over before this people, and he shall cause them to inherit the land which you will see."
>
> —DEUTERONOMY 3:23–28

LEAD AND SUCCEED

It is important to hold fast to decisions where you have applied nega-tive consequences—especially when strong messages or principles are at stake. Moses had failed to follow God fully in one respect—striking the rock rather than speaking to it as He had commanded. God required complete obedience from Moses to relay the proper message to His people, so His punishment was severe and irrevocable.

Before his death, Moses reminded the people of his own situation and the effects of obedience and disobedience. (See Deuteronomy 4:1–40.) He was a credible source because he was suffering the effects of his own actions. People want equity in what happens to leaders and employees. If God had been lenient on Moses, His message would have been diluted—and worse, He would have shown more respect for Moses, which goes against His char-acter. (See Acts 10:34.) God expects much from those who have been given much (Luke 12:48), and this should cause us to continually evaluate our motives and conduct.

Live It

- Think carefully before applying negative consequences; don't make them so onerous you are tempted to change them in the future.

- Realize the difference between changing your mind on a negative consequence and mitigating some of the negative implications of the consequence.
  - Allowing Moses to enter the Promised Land would have discounted the importance of being fully obedient.
  - Letting Moses see the Promised Land helped to mitigate the negative impact to some extent, yet continued to reinforce the importance of obedience.
  - More than fourteen hundred years later, God fulfilled Moses's dream by allowing him to return to Earth and enter the Promised Land to meet with Elijah and Jesus on the Mount of Transfiguration. (See Matthew 17:1–3.)

186

Correct People Compassionately

- Allow people to speak with you about the situation because it will enable you to reinforce your expectations and keep communications flowing to help repair any damaged relationships.

- Resist the temptation to let appeals go on for too long and give false hopes of a change in your decision.

- Reinforce your expectations (for example, Moses was to support the transition of leadership to Joshua) because it is easy for people to be distracted or disheartened while enduring negative consequences.

See It

During her first year, a talented new employee hired out of graduate school had met or exceeded all of her performance goals. Halfway through her second year, however, she began struggling. Her performance was slipping quickly, and it appeared her attitude was behind it. Her supervisor needed to take action, so a probationary period was established. The two agreed to the specific performance goals she needed to meet to successfully complete the probation.

During the three-month probation, she failed to meet any of her goals. Her supervisor realized no amount of talent could make up for lack of heart, so he reluctantly terminated her employment. He needed to show to the employee, and the organization, that performance was critical. He also wanted to show compassion for the employee involved, so he paid for career counseling and then helped her land a coveted job with another international corporation. In addition, he carefully identified how he could improve his department's screening process for evaluating all future potential employees.

CONCLUSION

As a leader, you will never get away from the need to correct people. The Bible provides a number of examples to help you take the needed action with confidence, knowing you are applying ancient wisdom and techniques that work.

chapter fourteen

ADDRESS STRIFE AND RESISTANCE

Redirect ineffective behaviors with appropriate and considerate actions

I N A BUSINESS context, strife and resistance are a certainty, and as a leader, you need to be ready for them. Ignoring them—or working to actively avoid them—will not get you off the hook and may actually compound the problem. The Bible has guidance for leaders at these difficult times—guidance that shows how to address the problems and also how to do so in ways that show consideration for those involved.

PREPARE PEOPLE FOR THE FUTURE

These stories took place toward the end of Jesus's three-year ministry. All of the Gospels include similar passages to the ones here.

> Now while they were staying in Galilee, Jesus said to them, "The Son of Man is about to be betrayed into the hands of men, and they will kill Him, and the third day He will be raised up." And they were exceedingly sorrowful.
>
> —MATTHEW 17:22–23

> Now Jesus, going up to Jerusalem, took the twelve disciples aside on the road and said to them, "Behold, we are going up to Jerusalem, and the Son of Man will be betrayed to the chief priests and to the scribes; and they will condemn Him to death, and deliver Him to the Gentiles to mock and to scourge and to crucify. And the third day He will rise again."
>
> —MATTHEW 20:17–19

LEAD AND SUCCEED

These things I have spoken to you, that you should not
be made to stumble. They will put you out of the synagogues; yes, the time is coming that whoever kills you will
think that he offers God service. And these things they
will do to you because they have not known the Father
nor Me. But these things I have told you, that when the
time comes, you may remember that I told you of them.
And these things I did not say to you at the beginning,
because I was with you....

Therefore you now have sorrow; but I will see you again
and your heart will rejoice, and your joy no one will take
from you.

—JOHN 16:1–4, 22

A valuable tactic for addressing resistance is to prepare people in advance
for difficult situations. There are times when leaders know about upcoming
changes—some of which may be disruptive and viewed negatively. Even if
the changes are viewed positively, recognize that resistance follows disrup-
tion, so people can resist aspects of changes they want to see happen. (Test
this for yourself by thinking about a disruptive personal change you chose
to make, such as moving, changing careers, or going back to school, and
recall your responses to the disruptions.) People respond best when they
have some degree of understanding about what will happen. This approach
also gives people time to consider their feelings and develop responses
rather than simply react to the changes when they occur. Here, Jesus began
to communicate the pending events leading to His crucifixion and resurrection. Notice He talked about it on multiple occasions, with increasing levels
of detail, which shows how He attempted to move the disciples through the
denial that was natural for the situation. Follow Jesus's example, and you'll
help others to handle disruptive changes more constructively.

Live It

- Be aware that people are likely to have picked up subtle
  signals about pending changes (for example, unusual meet-

Address Strife and Resistance

ings, travel, body language) and may have right or wrong ideas about what is happening.

- Consider the potential responses people will have to these changes, for instance:
  - Excitement but without a good understanding of the work required
  - Concern about personal impacts
  - Denial or an expectation something can be done to change it
  - Mixed views: positive on some facets and negative on others
- Determine any sensitivities about communications and their timing.
  - For some changes, there are legal or prudent limits on what can be said and when (for example, mergers, very large transactions, gain or loss of a significant customer).
  - Some information may be ill advised to communicate (for example, expected numbers of people to be laid off).
- Identify the messages you can and should deliver and who can receive them.
- Communicate the messages in a way that invites feedback and questions; look for indications of your expected responses, and recognize that not seeing those responses may be an indication of denial.
- Answer questions openly and honestly, not being reticent to say, "I don't know," or "Here are the possibilities, but I don't know which one is most likely."
- Use questions to test for understanding—and pose questions people may be uncomfortable asking.

LEAD AND SUCCEED

- Give people opportunities to get involved wherever possible; even when the news is negative, people often want to help, and it can be good for both them and the organization.

- Repeat the messages over time with the ultimate goal of:
  - Instilling realistic expectations when the changes are viewed positively
  - Gaining acceptance, although not necessarily agreement, when the changes are viewed negatively

- Acknowledge that major change is likely to be a mixed bag of positive and negative elements; expect a mixed response, and develop your messages, plans, and goals accordingly.

See It

Early one year, I began to pick up on subtle clues something big was happening. My boss was getting harder to reach, and on several occasions, her assistant mentioned casually she was in a city where I was unaware of any current business. A short time later, our leadership team was quickly assembled for an unscheduled conference call. We were all asked to sign nondisclosure agreements—then the announcement came.

We were going to acquire a small consulting firm and merge it into our business unit, doubling the size of our immediate group. After we discussed the limited details available at the time, we were all asked to provide support to the integration process. Following the initial announcement, a series of additional calls, confidential communications, and plans enhanced our understanding of the upcoming changes. This upfront notice gave me time to think about the impact on my department—to consider the likely questions and concerns and appropriate responses. It also gave me time to consider my own thoughts and feelings, which were admittedly mixed. As the process proceeded, I engaged actively in designing aspects of the integration and found it helpful for my own acceptance and understanding of the implications. It also helped me build relationships for working effectively in the newly integrated organization.

BEWARE OF STRIFE

Abraham and Sarah were the grandparents of Jacob, the father of the twelve tribes of Israel. Abraham and Sarah received their son Isaac by promise from God in their old age. Before Isaac was born, Sarah asked Abraham to bear a son for her through Hagar, Sarah's maid. This story takes place after Isaac was born.

> And Sarah saw the son of Hagar the Egyptian, whom she had borne to Abraham, scoffing. Therefore she said to Abraham, "Cast out this bondwoman and her son; for the son of this bondwoman shall not be heir with my son, namely with Isaac." And the matter was very displeasing in Abraham's sight because of his son. But God said to Abraham, "Do not let it be displeasing in your sight because of the lad or because of your bondwoman. Whatever Sarah has said to you, listen to her voice; for in Isaac your seed shall be called. Yet I will also make a nation of the son of the bondwoman, because he is your seed." So Abraham rose early in the morning, and took bread and a skin of water; and putting it on her shoulder, he gave it and the boy to Hagar, and sent her away. Then she departed and wandered in the Wilderness of Beersheba.
>
> —GENESIS 21:9–14

When there is a merger, change in leadership, or simply personality clashes, strife can result—and it will detract from the job at hand. Even if the actions to address strife are extremely difficult for you, be swift to take them. First take action to enable the relationships to work, but don't hesitate to reassign or remove the individual(s) if the strife continues, because other relationships and the organization's goals are in jeopardy. Your dedication to doing what is best for the organization and for the individuals involved, even if the near-term situation seems especially tough, will be good for everyone in the end.

LEAD AND SUCCEED

Live It

- Be alert to situations that tend to produce strife, including:
    - Changes to roles and responsibilities, such as new leadership
    - Organizational restructures, mergers, acquisitions, and partnerships where groups of people need to combine work efforts
    - Instances where strong personalities are vying for power
- Stay engaged so you can uncover the early signs of strife.
- Ask questions to understand the interactions between people and to uncover issues that need to be addressed.
- Communicate your expectations for effective teamwork and offer support (for example, teaming exercises, one-on-one coaching, facilitation).
- Take decisive action to address the source of the strife, and communicate the reasons for your actions if they are visible to others.

See It

A large company acquired a small firm that complemented and expanded one of its divisions. The leadership team for the newly merged division included leaders from both companies because leveraging the best of both was viewed as necessary for the business case. But a couple of the leaders were resistant to some changes—and it was apparent in their attitudes and interactions with others. The division executive chose to remove the leaders to address the strife, but he did so without discussions or other attempts to resolve the underlying concerns, which many viewed as valid. Although the executive showed appropriate concern for strife, his approach ultimately increased concern among members of the combined leadership team. The executive failed to act on the issues and did not explain his reasoning, so people heard one side of the story—from those who were removed. Several leaders chose to leave following this situation, expressing concern about their

194

Address Strife and Resistance

own careers. The loss of key leaders had a negative impact on the division, and the business case for the acquisition failed to reach its full potential.

SELECT TIMES TO INTERVENE

This episode happened shortly before Jesus was crucified and resurrected. Directly after this passage, Judas Iscariot is recorded as having approached the chief priests about betraying Jesus.

> And when Jesus was in Bethany at the house of Simon the leper, a woman came to Him having an alabaster flask of very costly fragrant oil, and she poured it on His head as He sat at the table. But when His disciples saw it, they were indignant, saying, "Why this waste? For this fragrant oil might have been sold for much and given to the poor." But when Jesus was aware of it, He said to them, "Why do you trouble the woman? For she has done a good work for Me. For you have the poor with you always, but Me you do not have always. For in pouring this fragrant oil on My body, she did it for My burial. Assuredly, I say to you, wherever this gospel is preached in the whole world, what this woman has done will also be told as a memorial to her."
> —MATTHEW 26:6–13

As leaders, it is vital to walk a fine line between intervening too rapidly and allowing issues to fester. Here, the majority was critical of the actions of one person, and it appears from the text the majority might have been scolding the woman. Jesus did not simply point out the problem and ask them to handle it themselves, as He did at other times. That would have been futile, since the majority would have "won." Instead, He intervened directly to stop the strife and explained another side of the situation the majority was not seeing. Without this explanation, the situation could have arisen again. Be selective in engaging the issues you see among people. Your choices of when and how to intervene can greatly impact what people will do in the future.

195

LEAD AND SUCCEED

Live It

- When issues arise, seek to understand who is involved and why the issues exist.

- Consider how similar issues have arisen and been resolved in the past.

- Determine if the issue is likely to be resolved on its own, and if so, be patient and monitor progress.

- If the issue is likely to fester, intervene as appropriate, considering whether the issue is based in:
  - Lack of information, where communications can be valuable
  - Inappropriate perspective or perceptions, where probing questions can be used to uncover and redirect thinking
  - Lack of knowledge or skill, where education or training may be required
  - Lack of motivation, where positive and negative consequences may be helpful

See It

"This issue won't go away on its own," I said as I met with a team on a complex project. Members of two project subteams were sniping at one another, and it was impeding progress. There was "history" between some of the people, and the problem was compounded by conflicting requirements and the natural checks and balances in business.

As we discussed how to help the teams overcome the rift, we decided not to ask their managers to intervene because it would be viewed as punitive. Instead, we agreed to do a little education and help them understand the source of their conflicts. "Let's discuss 'chartered conflict.' Chartered conflict happens when the work assignments of different groups conflict. It's not the people. It's not even bad—unless the people let it become personal..." That launched a working exercise to help the teams understand the issues and work out a better way to interact with each other. In a short time, a

196

Address Strife and Resistance

better, more constructive working relationship resulted. They didn't become friends, but the strife abated and the work was accomplished.

SQUELCH COMPLAINTS THROUGH DELEGATION

This story comes from a time early in the building of the Christian church, shortly after Jesus's resurrection and ascension.

> Now in those days, when the number of the disciples was multiplying, there arose a murmuring against the Hebrews by the Hellenists, because their widows were neglected in the daily distribution. Then the twelve summoned the multitude of the disciples and said, "It is not desirable that we should leave the word of God and serve tables. Therefore, brethren, seek out from among you seven men of good reputation, full of the Holy Spirit and wisdom, whom we may appoint over this business; but we will give ourselves continually to prayer and to the ministry of the word." And the saying pleased the whole multitude. And they chose Stephen, a man full of faith and the Holy Spirit, and Philip, Prochorus, Nicanor, Timon, Parmenas, and Nicolas, a proselyte from Antioch, whom they set before the apostles; and when they had prayed, they laid hands on them.
>
> —Acts 6:1–6

In this passage, people had a complaint. The leaders properly resisted the trap of jumping in to address the problem or direct the details of the answer. Instead, they identified a plan and delegated the execution details to the people with the complaint. Notice the leaders established boundaries for the proper answer, which in this case was the characteristics of the candidates for the job. The leaders were also involved in approving the selections made, which is another form of boundary. This answer resolved the problem quickly, and even the people with the complaint were pleased. Use involvement and delegation as techniques for addressing complaints. You may be amazed at how well—and how fast—they work!

LEAD AND SUCCEED

Live It

- Ask questions to further your understanding of the complaint.

- Resist the urge to become defensive if the complaint involves you or any of your previous decisions.

- Determine how you can assign the issue to others—especially the people who have raised the complaint.

- Remember it is vital to identify appropriate boundaries and requirements for the final solution: the criteria by which you will accept the solution offered.

- Review and approve the final design or decision; be careful about requiring too many changes to the design because it may reduce commitment or indicate defensiveness on your part.

See It

I am a firm believer in open-book management—the practice of openly communicating financial details broadly across organizations. When I took over an intact department, I sought help in establishing a good approach to open-book management from a good friend and expert in the topic, Chuck Kremer. Chuck recommended an approach for sharing success stories, setting goals, and tracking actions along with in-depth review of the financial statements. These steps consumed nearly an hour a month—taking over the agenda for one of our weekly meetings. But I was dedicated to the approach and was seeing many benefits.

About six months into the process, I sought feedback and was surprised at what I heard. Although they saw value in the process, several people expressed it took too long and involved too many steps. When I took a poll, others agreed. So I asked those most vocal to take on a project to improve the process. I gave the team a few boundaries and sent them off. The results were wonderful. The process was streamlined and allowed for other topics during those staff meetings. Also, the team had gathered broad input across

198

Address Strife and Resistance

the department, so everyone was committed to the new process, and we gained even more benefits.

REPEAT KEY INSTRUCTIONS AND EXPECTATIONS

The Bible documents several people whose names were changed, including Simon to Peter, Saul to Paul, and Jacob to Israel. These episodes document the changing of Jacob's name to Israel, which occurred later in his life.

> [The Man] asked him, What is your name? And [in shock of realization, whispering] he said, Jacob [supplanter, schemer, trickster, swindler]! And He said, Your name shall be called no more Jacob [supplanter], but Israel [contender with God]; for you have contended and have power with God and with men and have prevailed.
>
> —GENESIS 32:27–28, AMP

> And God [in a distinctly visible manifestation] appeared to Jacob again when he came out of Padan-aram, and declared a blessing on him. Again God said to him, Your name is Jacob [supplanter]; you shall not be called Jacob any longer, but Israel shall be your name. So He called him Israel [contender with God]....Then Israel journeyed on and spread his tent on the other side of the tower of Edar.
>
> —GENESIS 35:9–10, 21, AMP

As a leader, expect that you will need to repeat key instructions multiple times. Here, God's instruction for Jacob to be renamed Israel was not fulfilled for several chapters—perhaps representing many years. In fact, the name Israel seemed to stick only late in his life. It is important to follow up on your key instructions to ensure the message is received. If your expectations are not being fulfilled, communicate your instructions again. Then be sure to look for and remove any barriers getting in the way of your expectation.

LEAD AND SUCCEED

Live It

- Expect to repeat key instructions multiple times, especially when they are complex, are significantly different from what is currently happening, or involve multiple people.

- Plan your communications to use multiple methods, different phraseology, and examples.

- Use questions to ensure your messages have been received.

- Monitor progress, being patient particularly in the beginning.

- Meet one-on-one with people to understand any barriers that may exist.

- Continue to monitor and support progress until your instructions are fulfilled.

See It

"They've had two years to get this. What is the matter with these people?" An executive sponsor for a major transformation effort vented his frustration. His lead consultant had just communicated the results of a study that indicated some people were still questioning whether the solution would work despite a number of early successes. The project team felt the communications were adequate. By then, people had received multiple messages from many directions, including from the executive sponsor who was determined to make it work. It was clear the executive's frustration was nearing a peak, and he was contemplating strong actions that could make the transformation more difficult in the long run.

The project team devised a last-ditch effort: meet one-on-one with people who expressed doubts and provide them with additional information and education, especially about early successes. They used a tactic called "reality testing." After the additional information was communicated, most people were sold on the vision—and it was clearer where the communications process needed to be enhanced. For people who continued to express doubts, the first stage of reality testing kicked in. "You know, the executive sponsor truly wants—and needs—you to support and drive this program.

200

Address Strife and Resistance

We're here to help you do that. Right now, you're not helping like we need you to help..." For most of the doubters, that was all it took. They asked how they could become more involved, especially in making adjustments to make it successful.

But a few others needed the second stage. After even more information to answer their concerns, they were told, "Frankly, I've got to tell you, the executive sponsor is losing patience. I'd do you a disservice if I didn't tell you that questioning the vision is not wise at this point. We know we need to make adjustments, and we want your help. But the next person you'll be talking to is the executive sponsor..." These additional messages, and the extra attention, were what it took to get the entire group pulling for the vision and working on the adjustments needed for success.

DEAL CAREFULLY WITH WILLINGNESS ISSUES

Jonah was a Jewish prophet who lived around 800–750 B.C. Nineveh, the city where he was called to preach, was a city of Gentiles. The entire Book of Jonah is a perfect example of how to handle a willingness issue—an especially difficult leadership challenge. For this reason, throughout the passages below, notes are included to highlight how God handled each stage. To get full benefit, you are strongly encouraged to read the entire Book of Jonah.

> Now the word of the LORD came to Jonah the son of Amittai, saying, "Arise, go to Nineveh, that great city, and cry out against it; for their wickedness has come up before Me."
> —JONAH 1:1–2

God made His expectations for Jonah clear so there could be no misunderstanding. Also, Jonah was able to perform God's task for him. If you encounter a willingness issue, start by ensuring the expectations are clear and the person has the necessary capabilities.

> But Jonah arose to flee to Tarshish from the presence of the LORD. He went down to Joppa, and found a ship going to Tarshish; so he paid the fare, and went down into it, to go with them to Tarshish from the presence of the LORD.

201

LEAD AND SUCCEED

> But the LORD sent out a great wind on the sea, and there
> was a mighty tempest on the sea, so that the ship was about
> to be broken up.
>
> —JONAH 1:3–4

When it was clear the assignment was not being fulfilled, God applied negative consequences. Read verses 7–15, and you'll see it was clear to Jonah his problems were due to resistance—and they were getting worse.

> Now the LORD had prepared a great fish to swallow Jonah.
> And Jonah was in the belly of the fish three days and three
> nights.
>
> —JONAH 1:17

Even though Jonah attempted to control the situation by getting the sailors to throw him overboard, God simply changed the negative consequences to fit his new situation. In other words, God continued to apply pressure to get Jonah to do what was needed. This can be the toughest part of dealing with a willingness deficiency: staying the course. But if you let up at this point, people will learn resistance can be successful.

> Then Jonah prayed to the LORD his God from the fish's belly.
> And he said: "I cried out to the LORD because of my afflic-
> tion, and He answered me. Out of the belly of Sheol I cried,
> and You heard my voice."
>
> —JONAH 2:1–2

God kept the channels of communication open throughout the process of applying negative consequences.

> "But I will sacrifice to You with the voice of thanksgiving;
> I will pay what I have vowed. Salvation is of the LORD." So
> the LORD spoke to the fish, and it vomited Jonah onto dry
> land.
>
> —JONAH 2:9–10

202

Address Strife and Resistance

As soon as Jonah indicated he would perform the required task, the negative consequences were removed.

> Now the word of the LORD came to Jonah the second time, saying, "Arise, go to Nineveh, that great city, and preach to it the message that I tell you."
>
> —JONAH 3:1

With willingness expressed, God reconfirmed His expectations.

> So Jonah arose and went to Nineveh, according to the word of the LORD.... Then God saw their works, that they turned from their evil way; and God relented from the disaster that He had said He would bring upon them, and He did not do it.
>
> —JONAH 3:3, 10

God monitored the situation and ensured Jonah's work was completed.

> But it displeased Jonah exceedingly, and he became angry. So he prayed to the LORD, and said, "Ah, LORD, was not this what I said when I was still in my country? Therefore I fled previously to Tarshish; for I know that You are a gracious and merciful God, slow to anger and abundant in lovingkindness, One who relents from doing harm. Therefore now, O LORD, please take my life from me, for it is better for me to die than to live!" Then the LORD said, "Is it right for you to be angry?"
>
> —JONAH 4:1–4

God's earlier emphasis on open communications became vital when the original reason for resistance reemerged. Frequently people will exhibit an emotional response after being required, through pressure, to complete something they are not willing to do.

LEAD AND SUCCEED

> And the LORD God prepared a plant and made it come up
> over Jonah, that it might be shade for his head to deliver him
> from his misery. So Jonah was very grateful for the plant.

—JONAH 4:6

Beginning in Jonah 4:6–10, you will see God did not simply stop at the completion of the task. He followed up with Jonah on a personal level. This vital step is often overlooked, yet it sends a clear message that the person is important and the leader is not interested solely in results. It is also a chance for the leader to reinforce priorities and philosophy, which may help prevent future willingness problems. This part of Jonah's story could have been easily left out of the Bible—God's will had been carried out. However, restoring the relationship is approximately 25 percent of the story.

Jonah demonstrates a pure willingness deficiency. He was fully able to perform God's task, and there is no indication he believed it was not worthwhile. He simply did not want to see Nineveh relieved from its impending destruction. The process God followed is called consequence management: the application of positive or negative consequences based on whether or not instructions are performed. Consequence management is appropriate after other actions have failed, including communication, training, and providing additional support. The basic steps are to clarify requirements, apply increasing consequences (for example, either remove positives or add negatives), stay the course, and restore the relationships—all the while keeping communications open. Reread the story of Jonah when you face a willingness issue. It provides all the steps to handle it successfully.

Live It

- Ensure your expectations are clear.

- Open and maintain a two-way dialogue to uncover the source of resistance, and apply the appropriate response.

- Recognize resistance can come from multiple sources (for example, concerns over needed capabilities and resources to perform the work, view that the rewards are insufficient); be

204

Address Strife and Resistance

sure to discover the real reason so you can apply the right response.

- Resist the temptation to jump too quickly to pressure tactics because they can erode relationships and loyalty when over-used or inappropriately applied.

- If negative consequences are warranted, recommunicate your expectations along with the consequence for failing to perform.

- Be prepared for a partial response, and be determined not to settle for it.

- Apply your communicated consequences along with a message of how they can be removed.

- Stay the course and apply increasing consequences if appropriate.

- As soon as the person indicates agreement to comply, remove the consequence (don't wait until the work is done); then monitor performance and reapply consequences if necessary.

- After the requirements are fulfilled, meet with the person to resolve any relationship issues—and reconfirm your interest about the person, his or her career, and so on.

- Continue to monitor the relationship and results for a time to guard against lingering issues.

See It

On a major transformation effort, one of the senior managers was not on board. He was openly negative about the initiative—even with staff—and was not taking the needed action to engage his business unit adequately in the work. The project executive met with him repeatedly to address the issue, but he finally raised the problem with the sponsoring executive. The sponsoring executive met with the senior manager, and immediately the project executive noticed a huge improvement. The senior manager began doing the needed work—and even "changed his tune" when speaking with others.

205

LEAD AND SUCCEED

After a few weeks, when it was clear the change was going to stick, the project executive met with him and asked about it. "I'm thrilled you are on board now. It's making a huge difference. What happened?" The senior manager mentioned his meeting with the sponsoring executive. "We discussed the vision, the reasons we need to make the change, and what I need to do to support it." The project executive didn't let up. "Well, we discussed all these things too when we met." The senior manager nodded and added, "Yes, we did. But you didn't explain it the same way he did." Clearly the senior manager was referencing the negative consequences—stated or implied—facing him if he continued to resist. It was the right message at the right time—delivered by the right person. And it worked.

CONCLUSION

The Bible gives business leaders a number of great examples for dealing with the difficult issues of strife and resistance. Most of these situations require a careful balance of being proactive, yet not engaging too quickly or strongly—obviously an opportunity for prayer to get it right! Even though you're not likely to ever enjoy dealing with these issues, there are ways to handle them without undue stress by following the approach God has made available to us.

chapter fifteen

GUARD YOUR HEART
Live a leader-worthy life

I N ALL THINGS in life, both *what* we do and *why* we do it are important. It is not enough to simply do the right thing. You need to take action with the right motives to be fully right. Even further, right motives can cover a multitude of *what* problems—issues caused despite the best of intentions. The best single proof may be the life of David. David was far from perfect as a military leader, king, husband, and father. The proof? How about infidelity, murder, and family problems, just to name a few. However, his heart was intent on following God, as recorded in Acts 13:22. Leading from your heart—with continual emphasis on right motives—will make you a more successful business leader.

REMEMBER LEADERSHIP IS LONELY AT DIFFICULT TIMES

This scripture recounts an event shortly before David became king over Israel. David found himself not only handling an extremely emotional and difficult situation but also one where his followers had turned against him.

> Now it happened, when David and his men came to Ziklag, on the third day, that the Amalekites had invaded the South and Ziklag, attacked Ziklag and burned it with fire, and had taken captive the women and those who were there, from small to great; they did not kill anyone, but carried them away and went their way. So David and his men came to the city, and there it was, burned with fire; and their wives, their sons, and their daughters had been taken captive. Then David

LEAD AND SUCCEED

and the people who were with him lifted up their voices and wept, until they had no more power to weep. And David's two wives, Ahinoam the Jezreelitess, and Abigail the widow of Nabal the Carmelite, had been taken captive. Now David was greatly distressed, for the people spoke of stoning him, because the soul of all the people was grieved, every man for his sons and his daughters. But David strengthened himself in the LORD his God.

—1 SAMUEL 30:1–6

There are times when there is simply no one else to turn to other than God. All of us will face challenges in our work life, some of which may be extreme, such as bankruptcy or the death of workers. At times like this, people may turn on their leaders and respond angrily. For this reason, it is important to cultivate the ability to strengthen yourself for the work that needs to be done. Notice David didn't strengthen himself in himself, but rather he strengthened himself in the Lord his God. David's relationship with God enabled him to get through. If you follow this story through the end of chapter 30, you'll find all was restored. Had David reacted without trusting in God, the story may have had a different ending.

Live It

- Keep yourself emotionally prepared for the unexpected through spending regular time reading the Bible and in prayer.

- Recognize, as the leader, you have a greater responsibility than others at difficult times; be quick to set aside your emotional reactions to rapidly take action.

- Initiate communications quickly after a problem has arisen, and dedicate yourself to frequent communications throughout because people will want to see and hear from you.

Guard Your Heart

- Choose to trust God in prayer while you also consult advisers for wise counsel on what you should do.

See It

The director for a small business was very positive about an intern's ninety-day performance review. She was rapidly climbing a steep learning curve, and he was impressed. She was eager, enthusiastic, and well liked by others as well. Soon the director offered her a full-time position. She continued to perform well, and her reviews at six months and one year were equally positive.

However, shortly thereafter, her performance fell off—dramatically. The director met with her to uncover the reasons, and she shared that her engagement to be married had just been called off. She was crushed emotionally, and it was hard to keep her thoughts on her work. She promised the director she would snap out of it and do better. But that didn't happen. She often sat lifeless at her desk, obviously with her mind elsewhere. Her performance was not getting better, and in fact, she eventually shut down and produced no work at all.

The director had to do something. He knew the woman was well liked and that others felt sorry for her. But he needed to get the work done—and he needed to send a message about the importance of performance to others as well. He prayed and sought God about what to do. How he could handle the sensitive situation delicately yet properly? Eventually the director fired the woman—and suffered intense criticism as a result. He knew he was following God's leading, so he stayed encouraged that all would be fine in the end. He made special provisions to help the woman find another position—one that would be even better suited to her interests and career aspirations. He was right; it was fine in the end. Others eventually understood what he had done and why, and they appreciated the extra efforts he made to help her find a better position. The woman herself also appreciated the director's consideration, and they continued to stay in contact throughout their careers.

REMAIN CALM UNDER PRESSURE

This story of Jesus with His disciples occurred on the Sea of Galilee—a large lake in northern Israel. Some of the disciples—including Peter and

LEAD AND SUCCEED

Andrew—had made their living as fishermen there, so they knew the sea, and its storms, well.

> Now when He got into a boat, His disciples followed Him. And suddenly a great tempest arose on the sea, so that the boat was covered with the waves. But He was asleep. Then His disciples came to Him and awoke Him, saying, "Lord, save us! We are perishing!" But He said to them, "Why are you fearful, O you of little faith?" Then He arose and rebuked the winds and the sea, and there was a great calm. So the men marveled, saying, "Who can this be, that even the winds and the sea obey Him?"
>
> —MATTHEW 8:23–27

As leaders, it is important to remain calm under pressure. Jesus's faith allowed Him to be calm in a life-threatening situation. When we put our trust in God, it will lead to the faith we need to remain at peace even during the most challenging situations. Leaders who are calm are more likely to make effective decisions. Stress and fear can literally rob us of our ability to think and act properly. Also, others will be positively influenced by our confidence when we remain calm under pressure.

Live It

- Stay ready for unexpected problems in business through daily Bible reading and prayer; they will strengthen your faith and trust in God.

- Recognize that challenges from both work and your personal life can negatively impact your work.

- Remember that no problem—no matter how unexpected—is a surprise to God.

- Recognize that your initial reaction sets the tone for your emotions and responses, and also for others' reactions.

Guard Your Heart

- When confronted with a challenge, immediately ask for God's help in prayer; memorize 2 Timothy 1:7 so you have it "handy."

- Refrain from making decisions or taking action until you have an inner peace; read Philippians 4:6–7 and let it guide you.

- Learn from every experience—about how to avoid some problems and better deal with the unavoidable ones.

See It

A few short months after I bought a house, I discovered a structural defect. I believe it was God's guidance that led me to hire the engineer who had seen the problem before the sellers hired contractors to conceal it. The discovery led to fourteen months of extraordinary expense and disruptive repairs as well as legal wrangling. I was traveling back and forth five days a week to California on a challenging consulting engagement—and the emotions and stress of my personal situation, coupled with inadequate sleep, took a toll on me.

My consulting client was very satisfied with my work, which was my primary gauge of how well I was performing. However, I later learned my boss was not fully satisfied. My personal situation was apparent to him—and presumably to others as well. My review that year, although satisfactory, reflected his view I had let my personal problem impact my work life. At the time, I felt it was "unfair" because my client was satisfied, but with hindsight, I recognize I did not demonstrate calm under pressure. Although I was praying and seeking God, I was also trusting in my own efforts. This increased the stress I felt and let me give in to the emotions of the situation. The structural and legal issues were eventually resolved—not to anyone's satisfaction (except, perhaps, the contractor who fixed the problem). I learned how easily life can impact my business responsibilities and how I needed a stronger trust in God to remain calm in a storm.

LEAD AND SUCCEED

PRAY FOR OTHERS

The following verses are from a prayer by King Solomon for the people of Israel. The occasion was the dedication of the first temple.

> And may You hear the supplications of Your servant and of Your people Israel, when they pray toward this place. Hear from heaven Your dwelling place, and when You hear, forgive....
>
> Whatever prayer, whatever supplication is made by anyone, or by all Your people Israel, when each one knows his own burden and his own grief, and spreads out his hands to this temple: then hear from heaven Your dwelling place, and forgive, and give to everyone according to all his ways, whose heart You know (for You alone know the hearts of the sons of men), that they may fear You, to walk in Your ways as long as they live in the land which You gave to our fathers.
>
> —2 CHRONICLES 6:21, 29–31

Read Solomon's entire prayer for the people in 2 Chronicles 6:12–42.

Leaders who put their trust in God do well to pray for the people they lead—and for other business associates. This practice goes along with the view that leadership is a responsibility. Pray regularly for others. It will increase your compassion for them as well as open the opportunity to hear from God on their behalf.

Live It

- Recognize that prayer invites God to get involved in your work situation.

- Set aside time for daily prayer, and make sure your business associates are on the list—those you lead as well as your peers and leaders.

- Seek prayer partners you can pray with regularly.

212

Guard Your Heart

- Offer to pray for others when you become aware of problems in their lives; it may open additional opportunities to help them as well as demonstrate your concern and faith.

See It

A number of years ago, I was assigned to a consulting project for a company struggling financially. The company needed to significantly reduce its costs, which meant a number of difficult actions, including layoffs. As I walked by a bulletin board one day, I noticed a weekly prayer group announcement. The meeting was held at a café in town, and I showed up at the next meeting to the surprise of the "regulars" who did not expect to see a stranger join their group.

The company was a heavy manufacturer, so there I sat among welders and machine operators—all who loved God and were dedicated to seeking Him at that very difficult time. I told them I felt impressed to pray for them and their company, and they were pleased God had sent a believing, praying consultant to be a part of the team helping them. We prayed together for wisdom—and for God's will and His help. We also prayed for specific needs brought to the group. I participated in the prayer group until my assignment was complete, and I believe our collective faith was used by God in the company's eventual turnaround.

REMEMBER GREED IS DANGEROUS

These verses in Proverbs are a part of the instruction Solomon received from his parents. Apparently concerns over greed have been around for a long time!

> My son, if sinners entice you, do not consent....But [when these men set a trap for others] they are lying in wait for their own blood; they set an ambush for their own lives. So are the ways of everyone who is greedy of gain; such [greed for plunder] takes away the lives of its possessors.
> —Proverbs 1:10, 18–19, amp

LEAD AND SUCCEED

Over the years, a number of companies have succumbed to the greedy actions of leaders. By focusing on themselves and their own gain, these leaders have ruined their lives and reputations, and they have devastated the lives of many others. Those of us who desire to follow the Bible's wisdom may find ourselves working alongside people who have gotten to similar, and even higher, heights using approaches contrary to God's will. We must be very careful not to follow their example, but rather seek to be a godly influence in our work environments. Money is enticing, but God provides a better way for us—and true riches to seek.

Live It

- Stay constantly aware of the trap of greed; it is easy to fall into.

- Study the Bible's principles about money and giving to ensure you have the right attitude; for instance, read 1 Timothy 6:10 and 2 Corinthians 9:6–11.

- Check yourself:
  - Have you made decisions or taken actions because of the money you could make (or avoid losing)?
  - If so, what action would you have taken if money was not a factor?
  - What can you do to better handle such situations in the future?

- Study your reactions to others when it comes to the topic of money because they can signal a weakness in you or indicate a problem you are supposed to help solve.

See It

On one project, I advised a company against setting up an award program. The company used a number of monetary awards, believing it was the best way to get people to respond. But in this case, I felt it would send the wrong message and motivate people to take action for the wrong reasons.

The work involved a communication series for people to share their

214

Guard Your Heart

"lessons learned." We were working to motivate positive storytelling about a new capability they wanted to enhance and grow within the company. The communication series was designed for learning and sharing, so doing it for an award seemed like the wrong reason. Instead, we worked to generate a view that having your story selected was an honor in and of itself. We also requested executives to listen to the podcasts and send acknowledgments and thank-you notes to the storytellers to bolster the recognition—something that may have been harder to get them to do if they were giving out monetary awards.

After launching the series, we found many people eager to share their stories and that the executive responses were deeply prized. Also, the recognition from peers and simply being asked to contribute came to be viewed very positively. Money could not have replaced the value people gained from participating in the series and feeling appreciated by their leaders and peers.

REMEMBER THE GLORY IS GOD'S

King Solomon's wisdom is well known today—and it was also well known in his day. Here Solomon was visited by the queen of Sheba, who was enamored by the many blessings she saw in his life.

> Now when the queen of Sheba heard of the fame of Solomon, she came to Jerusalem to test Solomon with hard questions, having a very great retinue, camels that bore spices, gold in abundance, and precious stones; and when she came to Solomon, she spoke with him about all that was in her heart. So Solomon answered all her questions; there was nothing so difficult for Solomon that he could not explain it to her. And when the queen of Sheba had seen the wisdom of Solomon, the house that he had built, the food on his table, the seating of his servants, the service of his waiters and their apparel, his cupbearers and their apparel, and his entryway by which he went up to the house of the LORD, there was no more spirit in her.
>
> Then she said to the king: "It was a true report which I heard in my own land about your words and your wisdom.

215

LEAD AND SUCCEED

However I did not believe their words until I came and saw with my own eyes; and indeed the half of the greatness of your wisdom was not told me. You exceed the fame of which I heard. Happy are your men and happy are these your servants, who stand continually before you and hear your wisdom! Blessed be the LORD your God, who delighted in you, setting you on His throne to be king for the LORD your God! Because your God has loved Israel, to establish them forever, therefore He made you king over them, to do justice and righteousness."

—2 CHRONICLES 9:1–8

King Solomon's life was greatly blessed, and the queen of Sheba made it clear she knew the source of those blessings. People who decide to follow the Bible's wisdom will find their lives are blessed, and others notice it. In fact, I believe God often shows His goodness through our lives to draw others into His love. Notice the queen specifically mentioned the people Solomon led and how they were blessed by the wisdom working in his life. If the people under our leadership are not blessed and happy, there is something wrong, and we should consider our ways and make adjustments. And if they are blessed and happy, we need to be sure to give God the glory for the good in our lives—and in theirs.

Live It

- Remember your leadership will be reflected in the lives of others.

- Ask others what they see in your team—what your leadership is accomplishing—and ask God to help you make any needed adjustments.
  - Are the people viewed as capable—having what it takes to get the job done?
  - Is the team seen as producing good results? Are they doing so through appropriate means and right motives?

Guard Your Heart

- Do the people appear to enjoy each other and their work?

- Find creative ways to give into the lives of others; it may be a way for them to see God's goodness.

- Choose to give God the credit for results—both privately and publicly—to avoid the trap of pride.

See It

In 2005, I was approached to write a book about an IBM innovation. Tangible Culture was the result of several years of work, beginning with IBM's acquisition of PricewaterhouseCoopers Consulting in 2002. Shortly after leading the change and culture integration work for that acquisition, I transferred into IBM Service Research to hone the experience and further develop a "promising" capability that needed a lot of work. It was clear to me Tangible Culture was an answer to much prayer on a difficult initiative, and I wanted to give God the glory for it. I also wanted to bless others who had been involved or had relevant experience. So I invited twenty-seven contributing authors and even more sidebar contributors. It was a way to give into their lives—and I received an added benefit of their help to ensure the book's contents were solid.

When I submitted my manuscript for *Can Two Rights Make a Wrong? Insights from IBM's Tangible Culture Approach*, I was told my mention of active participation in my Christian church wasn't a common thing for business authors. I was asked: "Are you sure you want to include it?" I prayed and sought advice, and we eventually agreed the mention would stay. For me, it was a way to give God the glory for both the book and for the capabilities I knew He had given me the privilege to bring forward.

CONCLUSION

Our actions begin in our hearts—in the inner thoughts and motives that drive us to make decisions and carry them out. That is why guarding our hearts is so important to being an effective business leader. The Bible tells us about a number of topics to prepare our thoughts and hearts for the everyday challenges of leadership. Be determined to live a life worthy of the responsibility of leadership, and you'll be well on your way to fulfilling God's desire for you in your work!

afterword

THE LORD OR *MY* LORD?

I WAS RAISED IN a Christian home and come from a strong heritage of people who actively practiced their faith for many generations. My upbringing included regular church and Sunday school attendance, but something was missing even though I didn't know it.

Jesus was Lord—I knew that. I believed He was the Son of God, He lived a sinless life, and He died for our sins. I also believed He was raised from the dead and ascended into heaven. But something was still missing.

In my midtwenties, I came in contact with a direct question that showed me what was missing: "Have you made Jesus the Lord of your life?" I knew that Jesus was *the* Lord, but I had not yet made Him *my* Lord. In one moment, what was missing was added to my life, and I can emphatically say I have never regretted my decision, even for a moment.

I hope this short testimony will cause you to look back on your life. If you cannot name a moment when you accepted Jesus as *your* Lord, I encourage you to do it. Being a follower of Jesus Christ is not an easy path, but even difficult days with Jesus are easier than good days without Him. He is the truest friend you will ever have.

> *Dear heavenly Father, I acknowledge that I have sinned and need a Savior. Romans 10:9–11 says if I confess that Jesus is Lord and believe in my heart that God raised Him from the dead, I will be saved. Jesus, I choose You as my Lord and Savior today. God, show me the purpose You have for my life, and I'll live for You. Thank You for taking my sin away and showing me how to live my life for You. In Jesus's name I pray. Amen.*

NOTES

Preface

1.   Creflo Dollar, "Prosperity Overflow: Eight Steps to Your Destination" study notes, sermon preached August 14, 2005, http://creflodollarministries .org/Public/Bible/Study-Note.aspx?id=32&culture=EN (accessed February 17, 2009).

2.   Theodore Roosevelt, "Citizenship in a Republic," speech delivered at the Sorbonne, Paris, France, April 23, 1910, text accessed at Bartleby.com, http://www.bartleby.com/56/4.html (accessed February 17, 2009).

Chapter 3
Select the Right Leaders

1.   Sara Moulton Reger, *Can Two Rights Make a Wrong? Insights from IBM's Tangible Culture Approach* (Upper Saddle River, NJ: IBM Press, 2006), 67–83.

Chapter 10
Prepare Effective Communications

1.   Ibid.

2.   L. V. Gerstner, *Who Says Elephants Can't Dance? Inside IBM's Historic Turnaround* (New York: HarperCollins Publishers, 2002), 68–72.

3.   Moulton Reger, *Can Two Rights Make a Wrong?* 227–239.

BIBLIOGRAPHY

Barker, Kenneth, ed. *The NIV Study Bible, New International Version*. Grand Rapids, MI: Zondervan Publishing House, 1985.

Dake, Finis Jennings, ed. *Dake's Annotated Reference Bible*. Lawrenceville, GA: Dake Bible Sales, Inc., 1992.

Dollar, Creflo. "Prosperity Overflow: Eight Steps to Your Destination" study notes. August 14, 2005, http://creflodollarministries.org/Public/Bible/Study-Note.aspx?id=32&culture=EN.

Gerstner, L. V. *Who Says Elephants Can't Dance? Inside IBM's Historic Turnaround*. New York: HarperCollins Publishers, 2002.

Hayford, Jack W., ed. *The Hayford Bible Handbook*. Nashville, TN: Nelson Reference and Electronic (Thomas Nelson Publishers), 1995.

Moulton Reger, Sara. *Can Two Rights Make a Wrong? Insights from IBM's Tangible Culture Approach*. Upper Saddle River, NJ: IBM Press, 2006.

Roosevelt, Theodore. "Citizenship in a Republic." Speech delivered at the Sorbonne, Paris, France, April 23, 1910, http://www.bartleby.com/56/4.html.

The Amplified Bible. The Lockman Foundation. Grand Rapids, MI: The Zondervan Corporation, 1987.

ABOUT THE AUTHOR

SARA J. MOULTON Reger is a management consultant who specializes in organizational change management, culture transformation, governance, and leadership. Sara has been a management consultant since 1988 and has worked for IBM since 1995. Currently, she is the transformation program executive leading the culture and organizational change work and specific programs with IBM's technology outsourcing group. Before IBM, she worked for Deloitte Consulting, Ernst & Young, and StorageTek in the fields of management consulting and finance. Sara has an MBA concentrated in finance and management. She is a certified management accountant (CMA) and is also certified in the field of organizational change management.

Sara has a reputation for successfully leading the "people" side of difficult transformations and using those opportunities to develop practical methods and tools for future use. After leading the change and culture workstream for IBM's $3.5 billion acquisition of PricewaterhouseCoopers Consulting in 2002, Sara was asked to join IBM Service Research to hone and further develop the new techniques used to integrate thirty thousand new employees into an existing business unit of thirty thousand people. This innovation, now called Tangible Culture, is being used by IBM on its own transformation efforts and by IBM consultants globally with clients. Tangible Culture is documented in Sara's book *Can Two Rights Make a Wrong? Insights from IBM's Tangible Culture Approach*, published by IBM Press in 2006. Sara speaks frequently at conferences and has published on a variety of topics including business culture, business complexity, governance, e-business, communications, project risk management, change management, quality, and financial management.

LEAD AND SUCCEED

Sara lives in Scottsdale, Arizona, with her husband, Steve, and their kees-hond dogs, Racee and Roscoe. Both Sara and Steve are active in their church, Scottsdale First Assembly, and in studying the Bible daily. Sara enjoys music and photography and is a self-professed "wannabe" archeologist. She travels frequently for business and pleasure and looks forward to the day when she can follow in her parents' footsteps and travel the world. You may contact Sara at www.SaraMoultonReger.com.

FREE NEWSLETTERS
TO HELP EMPOWER YOUR LIFE

Why subscribe today?

- ☐ **DELIVERED DIRECTLY TO YOU.** All you have to do is open your inbox and read.

- ☐ **EXCLUSIVE CONTENT.** We cover the news overlooked by the mainstream press.

- ☐ **STAY CURRENT.** Find the latest court rulings, revivals, and cultural trends.

- ☐ **UPDATE OTHERS.** Easy to forward to friends and family with the click of your mouse.

CHOOSE THE E-NEWSLETTER THAT INTERESTS YOU MOST:

- Christian news
- Daily devotionals
- Spiritual empowerment
- And much, much more

SIGN UP AT: **http://freenewsletters.charismamag.com**